W9-BKY-005

"I urge you to read this pertinent book—and in Coach Wooden's words, 'discipline yourself so no one else has to.'"

Joe Maddon, Tampa Bay Rays manager

"I only spent three years at UCLA while Coach Wooden was still coaching, but I received a lifetime of positive influence from being around him. I leaned on what I learned from him many times throughout my career. Being able now to pick up Pat Williams's new book, *Coach Wooden*, and refresh my memories of all the conversations I had with Coach Wooden is very stimulating to me. I'm positive that you will find this wonderful book as valuable and powerful as I have. Thank you, Pat Williams!"

Dick Vermeil, former Philadelphia Eagles, St. Louis Rams,
and Kansas City Chiefs head coach

"John Wooden has had more influence on my coaching career than any other person. I have always admired the fact that John could tell you not only what he did as a coach but also why he did it and why it was important to do it that way, better than any other coach I have known. He will be remembered for his tremendous coaching accomplishments on the court but even more for his faith, his character, and the influence he had on so many other lives. I highly recommend Pat Williams's book."

Tom Osborne, University of Nebraska athletic director

"This book is about the early years of the greatest basketball coach who ever lived. John Wooden not only taught his players about basketball, he taught them how to live and appreciate life. He was a hero not just to basketball fans but to everybody. I respected John Wooden as a great coach but more importantly as a great man."

Tommy Lasorda, former Los Angeles Dodgers Hall-of-Fame manager

"We can never agree on who was the greatest player or coach in any sport, except for basketball. It's Coach Wooden, hands down. Even better, he was the best of all the great ones off the court. He had no equal, as you'll learn in this fascinating new book by his friend Pat Williams."

Jim Boeheim, Syracuse University head basketball coach

"Coach Wooden had retired from coaching before I was born, yet he is one of the coaches whom I have most admired and studied. He left a long-lasting mark, not only on the game but on all of us striving to be better leaders. This book will explain how he did it."

Brad Stevens, Butler University head basketball coach

"Coach Wooden has had a positive effect on my life, and after reading this book you will thank Pat Williams for keeping alive his philosophy and success principles."

Lou Holtz, former Notre Dame University and
University of South Carolina head football coach

"Coach Wooden's coaching philosophy has played a major role in my basketball career. Now you can learn about the foundation of his life in this important book by Pat Williams. Drop everything you're doing and start reading."

Mike Krzyzewski, Duke University head basketball coach

"Pat Williams has done a great job in capturing the essence of John Wooden—both the coach and the man. I enjoyed this book and you will too."

Sparky Anderson, former Detroit Tigers Hall-of-Fame manager

"Pat Williams has spent a lifetime studying the success principles of his friend John Wooden. This new book is loaded with Wooden wisdom that will deeply impact all of us."

Bill Parcells, Miami Dolphins executive
vice president of football operations

"I have read a lot of Coach Wooden's work, and it just makes so much sense to implement many of the principles that he has taught while he was coaching and during his retirement. This book may be the best of all."

Mark Richt, University of Georgia head football coach

"I have an enormous admiration for Coach Wooden and his coaching philosophy. This book adds great depth to the legend of Coach. You will enjoy it immensely."

George Karl, Denver Nuggets head coach

"John Wooden represented all the good qualities coaches are always teaching their young athletes. Coach Wooden was a master of getting people to perform at their maximum. This text will define why he was the greatest leader ever to grace the sidelines."

Dick Vitale, ESPN college basketball analyst

"I have known both Pat Williams and Coach Wooden for a number of years. No one could tell the story of the greatest coach of all time better than Pat."

Jim Calhoun, University of Connecticut head basketball coach

"Get ready for a terrific book based on the man who personified greatness and goodness. I loved Coach Wooden and you will too after reading this account of his life."

Dick Enberg, Hall-of-Fame sports broadcaster

COACH WOODEN

The **7** Principles That Shaped His Life
and Will Change Yours

PAT WILLIAMS
with JAMES DENNEY

Revell
a division of Baker Publishing Group
Grand Rapids, Michigan

© 2011 by Pat Williams

Published by Revell
a division of Baker Publishing Group
P.O. Box 6287, Grand Rapids, MI 49516-6287
www.revellbooks.com

Paperback edition published 2012
ISBN 978-0-8007-2127-5

Printed in the United States of America

All rights reserved. No part of this publication may be reproduced, stored in a retrieval system, or transmitted in any form or by any means—for example, electronic, photocopy, recording—without the prior written permission of the publisher. The only exception is brief quotations in printed reviews.

The Library of Congress has cataloged the original edition as follows:
Williams, Pat, 1940–
    Coach Wooden : the 7 principles that shaped his life and will change yours / Pat Williams with Jim Denney.
        p. cm.
    Includes bibliographical references.
    ISBN 978-0-8007-1997-5 (cloth)
    1. Christian life. 2. Success—Religious aspects—Christianity. 3. Wooden, John, 1910–2010. 4. Basketball fans—Religious life. I. Denney, Jim, 1953– II. Title.
    BV4598.3.W548 2011
    248.4—dc22   2010035619

Scripture marked KJV is from the King James Version of the Bible.

Scripture marked NIV is from the Holy Bible, New International Version®, NIV®. Copyright © 1973, 1978, 1984 by Biblica, Inc.™ Used by permission of Zondervan. All rights reserved worldwide. www.zondervan.com

12   13   14   15   16   17   7   6   5   4

In keeping with biblical principles of creation stewardship, Baker Publishing Group advocates the responsible use of our natural resources. As a member of the Green Press Initiative, our company uses recycled paper when possible. The text paper of this book is composed in part of post-consumer waste.

green press INITIATIVE

I gratefully dedicate this book
to Bill Bennett, longtime UCLA sports information
director and faithful John Wooden disciple.
This book never could have materialized without Bill's
insights, encouragement, and assistance.

Contents

Foreword

A Fine Legacy

The year was 1965, and Cazzie Russell and the Michigan Wolverines faced the UCLA Bruins in the NCAA finals. At the tender age of nine, I was a rabid Michigan basketball fan, and I thought Cazzie was invincible. I didn't know anything about UCLA or the Bruins coach, John Wooden, even though the Bruins had won their first NCAA title the previous year.

Well, Coach Wooden unleashed his Bruins, led by Walt Hazzard and Gail Goodrich. My dad and I listened to the game on the radio, and I couldn't believe what I heard: The Bruins crushed my beloved Wolverines 91–80, winning the NCAA championship for the second season in a row.

Over the years that followed, the legend of Coach John Wooden grew and grew. The Bruins not only won an incredible string of championships, but Coach Wooden's teams also produced scores of marquee players who went on to stardom in the NBA. My own college and pro career took me into football instead of basketball, but I continued to be fascinated by Coach Wooden's phenomenal success at UCLA. Each year, his roster would change and star players would graduate, yet the Bruins remained consistently successful. What was the *single* factor that *never* changed?

Coach John Wooden.

Whenever I read about Coach Wooden or saw him interviewed on TV, I could tell that there was an added dimension in his coaching style and his personality. He didn't just coach teamwork and preparation and strategy. He coached character and attitude and ideals. I remember being impacted by a little three-line poem my high school coach gave me, which was ascribed to Coach Wooden. Though Coach Wooden doesn't claim to have authored it, he certainly popularized it. The poem read:

> Talent is God-given: be humble.
> Fame is man-given: be thankful.
> Conceit is self-given: be careful.

After my playing career with the Pittsburgh Steelers, I went into coaching and became a student of Coach Wooden's coaching philosophy. I read everything that was written about him. I was impressed by the fact that Coach Wooden didn't just teach basketball—he taught *life*. He taught the fundamentals of good character, integrity, a strong work ethic, and teamwork—all the qualities necessary to success in life. He taught as much by his example as by his words. Though he was demanding and put his players through rigorous workouts, he was never personally demeaning, he never disciplined in anger, and he never used profane language.

Coach Wooden proved that you don't have to intimidate a player to motivate him or correct him. And while you are training your players' minds and bodies, don't forget to speak to their hearts. I was convinced that if the most successful coach in college basketball could be that kind of coach, then

I could find success in coaching football by remaining true to my values and my Christian faith. And that's what I set out to do.

I feel a great affinity with Coach Wooden. Like him, I was raised by parents who instilled in me the values and character qualities I needed for success—and like him, I was raised in the Christian faith. I'm the man I am because of my father, Wilbur, and my mother, Cleomae, both of whom were educators. Dad always taught me, "You don't have to do things the way other people do. If you go out and do it a different way, you'll become a leader."

A lot of people doubted that my style of coaching could win championships—but all of that changed after Super Bowl XLI. I thank God that I got the chance to prove it could be done—and I thank God for Coach Wooden, who led the way.

It has been fascinating to read this book by Pat Williams and to learn more about the seven-point creed that Joshua Hugh Wooden taught to his son Johnny so many years ago. These are the same values and principles my parents taught me in my formative years. It's instructive to see how John Wooden's father distilled these truths down to a seven-point creed, which continues to shape many lives today. By taking those seven truths and exploring them in depth, Pat Williams has performed a great service. Through interviews with dozens of John Wooden disciples, he has revealed scores of hidden facets of these seven great truths.

Like the rest of the sports world, I was saddened in June 2010 when I heard that Coach Wooden had passed away. He lived a long and full life, yet he was such a great soul that we wished we could keep him among us forever. Though he retired from basketball, he never stopped teaching, mentoring, and shaping lives. He continued living out those seven principles right to the end of his life.

John Wooden has left us, but the truths he taught us—and the truths his father taught him—still go on. That is a fine legacy for any man to leave.

Tony Dungy,
Super Bowl–winning NFL coach and author of *Quiet Strength*, *Uncommon*, and *The Mentor Leader*

Acknowledgments

With deep appreciation I acknowledge the support and guidance of the following people who helped make this book possible.

Special thanks to Rich DeVos, Bob Vander Weide, and Alex Martins of the Orlando Magic.

Hats off to my associates Andrew Herdliska and Latria Leak; my proofreader, Ken Hussar; and my ace typist, Fran Thomas.

Thanks also to my writing partner, Jim Denney, for his superb contributions in shaping this manuscript.

Hearty thanks also go to Andrea Doering, senior acquisition editor; Twila Bennett, senior director of marketing; and the entire Revell team for their vision and insight, and for believing that we had something important to say in these pages.

And, finally, special thanks and appreciation go to my wife, Ruth, and to my wonderful and supportive family. They are truly the backbone of my life.

Introduction

Well Done, Coach

During the first week of June 2010, my writing partner, Jim Denney, and I were preparing to put the finishing touches on this book. The chapters were mostly complete, and we were looking forward to finishing the final edits over the weekend. But on Wednesday of that week, my phone rang and I heard the voice of Coach Wooden's daughter, Nan.

"Pat," she said, "I wanted to let you know that my brother, Jim, and I have put Daddy in the hospital. We don't expect him to come out."

"Oh, Nan," I said, "I'm so sorry. I'll certainly be praying for Coach and for your family."

"Thank you. We just want him to rest comfortably and to be where he feels loved. He's very weak and frail. We're praying for him to go peacefully to be with Mother."

We talked for about twenty minutes about her father and about her grandfather Joshua Hugh Wooden and his seven-point creed. She shared with me a few memories of her grandfather.

"I left Martinsville when I was thirteen," she told me. "That was in 1948, when Daddy came to coach at UCLA. That was the last time I saw my grandfather, but I remember him well. There was always a comfort in my soul when I was with my grandfather. When I was small, he would read to me and rub my back.

"He had a strong faith in God, just like Daddy. My grandfather had high ideals, and he lived by them. He didn't preach at you; he just lived out his faith. I never heard him say an unkind word, and when you see someone live that way, it inspires you. It makes you want to be like him. I suppose that's why Daddy was so much like him."

Nan told me about Coach's first great-great-grandchild, who was not yet born. Little Charlie was due in August, and Coach had hoped to be on hand for Charlie's arrival. The lineage goes like this: Nan's daughter is Caryn; Caryn's daughter is Cori; Cori's son is Charlie—and Cori really wanted Coach and Charlie to meet each other.

But it was not to be. Coach went to be with the Lord—and with his beloved wife, Nell—on Friday evening, June 4, 2010. He is survived by his son, Jim; his daughter, Nan; his seven grandchildren; his thirteen great-grandchildren; and one soon-to-be-born great-great-grandchild.

A number of Coach's players and friends got to visit him in the final hours before he left us. One was Jamaal Wilkes, who went to see Coach on Thursday. After his visit, Jamaal reported, "Coach wanted to get up out of bed and shave. He said, 'I'm getting ready to go see Nellie.'"

The Sunday evening after Coach passed away was Game 2 of the NBA Finals between the Lakers and the Celtics in Los Angeles. At halftime, Kareem Abdul-Jabbar and Bill Walton talked about Coach Wooden's impact on their lives and their last good-byes with him.

"His impact was huge," said Kareem, who cut short a trip to Europe and flew home to see Coach one last time. "We thought he was teaching us the fundamentals of the game. But he was really teaching us life skills. He wanted us to be good citizens. He wanted us to be good parents. He wanted us to leave the university with a degree and to go out into the world and do meaningful things. He was such an effective teacher that it's hard to put that into perspective.

"I was really blessed that I made the choice to come to UCLA and have Coach Wooden mentor me and teach me during such an important part of my life. . . . Coach even taught me how to be a better parent. When I had children and I wondered how to deal with them, I would think back to how Coach would challenge us as players.

"When I went to see him at the hospital, he was under sedation, so I could only talk to him internally. But at least I got to see him and be with him, and he was still alive. He died only some three hours after I left him. But just to be in the same room with him and feel the family thing that was still happening around him—his children and grandchildren were there—it reminded me of what so much of my life has been about."

Bill Walton said, "Coach made me the player I was and the person I am. He was tough, he was firm, he was demanding, he was challenging—but he was fair and he made it fun. We could not wait to get to practice each and every day. What a grand celebration of life it was. He never came to practice and said, 'What do *you* guys want to do today?' He was the man in charge.

"The day I truly realized what Coach had meant in my life was the day I walked out of there. We had the pyramid of success, we had the seven-point creed, we had the two sets of threes, we had all the maxims and Woodenisms like, 'It's a game of skill, timing, and position. It's not a game of size and strength.' But when I walked out the door, after losing and failing and flopping in my senior year, he wrote a special maxim to me: 'Walton, it's the things you learn after you know it all that count.' I still have that to this very day.

"I had said my good-byes to Coach three months earlier. We both knew. But I had to see him one last time, so I went to the hospital on Tuesday to see him. He winced and said, 'Oh no, it's not you again!' And we laughed, and I told him one last time, 'Coach, thank you. I love you, and I'm sorry for all the consternation I caused you.'"

"Of Gentle Disposition . . ."

This book was written in the final year of Coach John Wooden's life. Only this introduction, the foreword, and the epilogue were composed after he passed away. That is why, throughout the pages that follow, I talk about him in the present tense. That is why all the players and friends I interviewed speak about him in the present tense. Coach was still living when these chapters were written.

I've decided to leave this book in the present tense. I made the decision not to go back and rewrite this book as if Coach were no longer with us. And part of the reason for that decision is something that one of Coach's players, Andy Hill, said about him. Andy told me, "He won't die. I've got him. Bill Walton's got him. We've all got him. He's not going anywhere."

And it's true. I've got him too. And so have you. I'm not going to write about him in the past tense, because he's still with us.

We've got his integrity. Coach was the same man, regardless of circumstances. He was consistent. His walk matched his talk. As one of Coach's former student managers told me, "Here's the deal with John Wooden: There was only one of him. The John Wooden on the practice floor was the same

John Wooden in the locker room. The John Wooden in the locker room was the same John Wooden on the campus. And the John Wooden on the campus was the same John Wooden at home."

We've got his wisdom, all the things he said and wrote and taught over the years. We've got his famous maxims, called "Woodenisms," which appear as sidebars throughout these pages, and which are collected in the appendix at the end of this book. We've got his example of faith, prayer, humility, gratitude, and caring for others. We've got him. He's not going anywhere.

Although I became personally acquainted with John Wooden only in the last decade, I first became aware of him in 1962, when I was a senior at Wake Forest and a catcher on the baseball team. That was the year our basketball team, with Len Chappell, Billy Packer, and Coach Bones McKinney, advanced to the Final Four. And that was also the first time Coach Wooden's UCLA Bruins made it to the Final Four.

Wake Forest lost to Ohio State in the national semifinal, then faced UCLA in the consolation game. (The Bruins had been defeated by eventual champion Cincinnati.) Wake Forest beat UCLA, but that game was Coach Wooden's last NCAA tournament loss for a long time. Over the next dozen years, Coach Wooden became the most successful coach in college basketball history, collecting eighty-eight consecutive wins, ten NCAA championships, and thirty-eight consecutive NCAA tournament victories.

Coach Wooden retired after the 1975 season and faded from public scrutiny for the next two decades. So many people in his position would have parlayed a record like his into a lucrative media and speaking career. But Coach Wooden's humility kept him out of the limelight. He didn't want to upstage any other coaches—and besides, he didn't think anybody really wanted to hear what he had to say.

I wish I had known. I wish I had looked him up and be-friended him during those twenty years of quiet semi-obscurity. I wish I had sought him out and asked him to mentor me and influence me as he had influenced so many people like Kareem and Bill Walton and Andy Hill and all the rest.

But fortunately for us all, while Coach was in his mideighties, a publisher sought him out and encouraged him to write a book. That book was *The Essential Wooden*, and with its publication, Coach Wooden and his ideas became wildly popular once more. As I studied Coach's wisdom, I was inspired to write a book called *How to Be like Coach Wooden*. Out of that project came my friendship with Coach, for which I will always be grateful.

I always looked forward to my visits with Coach Wooden. Every time I left his presence, I felt as if my soul had been scrubbed clean. I had the same experience in Coach's presence that Nan Wooden said she felt in the presence of her grandfather Joshua Hugh Wooden: There was always a comfort in my soul when I was with Coach.

After spending time with Coach Wooden, I always wanted to take my "game" to the next level. After being with him, I always wanted to ratchet up my faith, my prayer life, my integrity, and my wisdom. I wanted to be more like Coach. I wanted him to be proud of me. I wanted him to know how much he meant to me and how much he had impacted my life.

Coach Wooden and I lived three thousand miles apart, yet he has been a part of my life every day for years. I have studied his life, memorized his maxims, and interviewed hundreds of people who knew him. I can't get enough of Coach Wooden and his wisdom. And I can't get enough of his father, Joshua Hugh Wooden—a man so wise and so rich in insight that he formulated these seven life principles:

1. Be true to yourself.
2. Help others.

3. Make each day your masterpiece.
4. Drink deeply from good books, especially the Bible.
5. Make friendship a fine art.
6. Build a shelter against a rainy day by the life you live.
7. Pray for guidance and counsel, and give thanks for your blessings each day.

While I was working on this book, my friend Elmer Reynolds of Martinsville, Indiana, located a sixty-year-old copy of the *Martinsville Daily Reporter* from Wednesday, July 5, 1950, and faxed it to me. There on the front page was the obituary of Coach Wooden's father. The headline read, "J. Hugh Wooden Dies; Rites Today." The article spoke of his death after an illness of three weeks and said, "His four sons have been with them since the early part of his illness." The article also said, "For about fifteen years he had been employed at the Homelawn Sanitarium and was still there at the time he became ill."

Then, near the end of the obituary, there was this wonderful statement about the life of Joshua Hugh Wooden: "Of gentle disposition, Mr. Wooden had made many friends, and had always followed with great interest the athletic and teaching careers of his sons." What a great one-sentence eulogy for a life well lived. It speaks of the man's character, the esteem in which he was held, and his loving relationships with his sons. Of his father, Coach Wooden himself once wrote:

Joshua Hugh Wooden died long before the University of California—Los Angeles (UCLA) won a men's college basketball championship. Do I wish he'd lived to see me coach a team to a national title? Yes, but it wouldn't have mattered so much to him.

His priorities were different. Material things and public notice meant little. Education was important. Family was important. Outscoring someone in a basketball game, even for a national championship, had much less significance. Dad lived long enough to see me accomplish what was important to him. Nevertheless, he was responsible for the things that happened to me as a coach. Therefore, it surprises people that I received hardly any basketball instruction from Dad—no tips on jump shots, free throws, or anything else. He seldom attended games and was only slightly interested in results. His concern and guidance were deeper.[1]

And that statement about Joshua Hugh Wooden tells us a lot about Coach John Wooden and the impact he had on so many lives. The world celebrated this coach because of his victories and championships. But Coach's priorities were different. Material things and public notice meant little to Coach. Education was important. Family was important. His concern and guidance went far deeper than the game of basketball.

Like his father, Coach Wooden was a man of gentle disposition. Over his lifetime, he made many friends. And he always followed with great interest the lives and careers of the many young "sons" he mentored and coached. Like father, like son.

A Very Good Day

Saturday morning after Coach passed away, the mood was overcast at VIP'S Family Restaurant in Tarzana. The booth where Coach had breakfast every morning for the past fifteen years was empty. Somebody had placed flowers, a menu, and an 8 x 10 photo of Coach on his usual table. Even though the restaurant was full, no one sat at Coach's table. A sign marked the table reserved.

Things will never be the same at VIP'S.

But Coach wouldn't want his friends to be sad. He's right where he wants to be. He's home with Nell at last. He once wrote:

22

I was never preoccupied with dying. But perhaps like most people, I feared it. Losing Nell has cured me of any fear of death because I believe that when I'm called, when the Good Lord beckons according to His plan, I will go to heaven and be with her. Knowing this gives me peace.

Mind you, I'm in no hurry to leave, but I have no fear of leaving. When the time comes, it will be a very good day—Nell and I will be together again. In the meantime, each day of the journey is precious, yours and mine—we must strive to make it a masterpiece. Each day, once gone, is gone forever.

My father's words and deeds—his wisdom—taught me that and more.[2]

Coach Wooden's last appearance before an audience was in June 2008. He sat on the stage of the Nokia Theatre in Los Angeles with sports announcer Vin Scully and *L.A. Times* sports columnist T. J. Simers. During the evening, someone asked Coach, "When you get to the gates of heaven, what do you want to hear St. Peter say to you?"

In reply, Coach said simply, "Well done."

Well, Coach, you made it. That "very good day" has come. Thanks for all you taught us. Thanks for a life well lived.

God bless you, Coach. Well done.

1

A Common Man, a Leader's Leader

In July 2009, a blue-ribbon committee of sports experts helped the *Sporting News* rank the fifty greatest coaches of all time, in all sports. Number one on that list was John Wooden, the legendary head coach of the UCLA Bruins. His ten NCAA National Championships over twelve years is a record unmatched by any other coach in history. Even more amazing is the fact that seven of those championships occurred consecutively, and those seven championship seasons include an eighty-eight-game winning streak and four 30–0 undefeated seasons.

One of the great privileges of my professional sports career was to become personally acquainted with Coach. The more you study John Wooden, the more you realize that he is not only a *great* man—he's a *good* man. John Wooden is a man of character, wisdom, self-discipline, faith, integrity, honor, humility, and compassion for others.

There have been many books written about the life and philosophy of Coach John Wooden, but this is a book about the *foundation* of Coach's life—a simple seven-point creed. For well over a decade, I have been intensely studying the life of John Wooden. Like the Spanish explorer Juan Ponce de León in his search for the fountain of youth, I have been searching for the wellsprings of this man's greatness as a leader and a human being.

I've become convinced that both the greatness and the goodness of John Wooden can be traced to his father, Joshua Hugh Wooden. In fact, I believe the character and achievements of John Wooden can largely be traced to a piece of paper his father gave him on the day he graduated from the eighth grade at a little country grade school in Centerton, Indiana. Joshua Hugh Wooden was not a rich man, so the only gifts he could give his son that day were (as Coach later recalled) "a two-dollar bill, and a small card with a poem on one side and seven rules for living on the other."[1] The poem was a verse by Henry Van Dyke:

> Four things a man must learn to do
> If he would make his life more true:
> To think without confusion clearly,
> To love his fellow-man sincerely,
> To act from honest motives purely,
> To trust in God and Heaven securely.[2]

The seven rules that Joshua Hugh Wooden wrote on the other side of the paper were:

1. Be true to yourself.
2. Help others.
3. Make each day your masterpiece.
4. Drink deeply from good books, especially the Bible.
5. Make friendship a fine art.
6. Build a shelter against a rainy day by the life you live.
7. Pray for guidance and counsel, and give thanks for your blessings each day.

As Joshua Wooden handed that piece of paper to twelve-year-old Johnny, he said very simply, "Son, try to live up to this." John Wooden placed that piece of paper in his wallet and has kept it with him throughout his life. Not only that, but he even kept the two-dollar bill his father gave him. Decades later he handed it down to his own son, Jim Wooden.

Denny Crum, a former UCLA assistant under John Wooden and longtime basketball coach at Louisville, told me, "Coach has carried the original piece of paper with the seven-point creed his whole life. I've seen him take the paper out of his wallet, where he's kept it safe for going on ninety years. The paper is almost impossible to read because it's been folded for so long. It's a slip of white silky paper and looks almost like a piece of parchment. It's amazing to think that the little document his dad gave him is still around."

Even more amazing is the impact of that little document on John Wooden's life. "That seven-point creed," Denny added, "has served as a guideline for Coach his entire life, and he honors those guidelines to the best of his ability. They really are a way of life for Coach. I've never seen him do anything that would dishonor his father or his family. He had a world of respect for his dad. Joshua Wooden was the big inspiration in Coach's life."

In my own study of John Wooden's life, I had come to the same conclusion. In fact, I am convinced that much of Coach Wooden's amazing success as a coach, a leader, and an influence on young lives can be traced to the simple words his father wrote on that piece of paper so many years ago.

My Introduction to Joshua Hugh Wooden

I've long been familiar with central Indiana because I attended Indiana University from 1962 to 1964, while working on my master's degree. During those years, I fell in love with these wonderful people who call themselves "Hoosiers." I loved the small towns and the farmlands and the scenery of Indiana, but I had never visited Martinsville, the hometown of the greatest coach in sports history.

One of my favorite Hoosiers is a lifelong resident of Martinsville named Elmer Reynolds. He is a huge admirer of Coach Wooden, and he became an enthusiastic supporter of the book I was writing at the time, *How to Be like Coach Wooden*. He invited me to Martinsville and said, "I'll take care of all the details."

So in 2004, I flew to Indiana. With Elmer's help, I gathered everybody available who had known Coach Wooden—old-timers, distant relatives, friends, and neighbors. It was an eclectic group, and we met in Poe's Cafeteria, Coach Wooden's favorite little restaurant in Martinsville. We spent the better part of the day together. The good people of Martinsville shared hundreds of memories of John Wooden and his family, and I wrote down every detail. It was a marvelous day.

At the end of that session, I said to Elmer, "Is there anything else I should do in Martinsville before I leave?"

"Oh, yes. Let me round out the rest of your itinerary."

So Elmer and I left Poe's Cafeteria, and he took me to the historic high school gymnasium where John Wooden played basketball in the late 1920s. The building had been slated for demolition in the late 1970s, but wiser heads had prevailed and the town had restored and renovated this red-brick basketball palace instead of tearing it down. I remembered what Coach Wooden had said about Indiana basketball in those days: Hoosiers were just crazy about the game. Back when Johnny Wooden played high school basketball, a sign at the edge of town proclaimed the population of Martinsville to be forty-eight hundred people. Well, that old gymnasium seated fifty-two hundred—the entire population of Martinsville plus four hundred more.

Next, Elmer and I drove out to the suburbs of Martinsville, to the farm where Coach grew up. The Wooden family farmhouse is still there. It is very small but in good repair (a brick porch has been added since Coach lived there), and it is surrounded by fields of tall green corn. The narrow dirt lane that used to pass by the Wooden family farmhouse is now Centerton Road, a wide, paved, two-lane road.

I stood on the side of that road in front of the house where John Wooden once lived, and Elmer snapped pictures. The house is probably wired for cable TV and the Internet today, but when Coach lived there, the house didn't even have electricity, running water, or indoor plumbing. I looked but could see no sign of the old outhouse that used to stand behind the house. (Coach called it a "three-holer," so it must have been a truly deluxe privy!)

Next, Elmer took me to the cemetery where Coach Wooden's parents were buried. There we found the gravesites of Joshua Hugh Wooden and Roxie Anna Wooden, Coach's father and mother. Elmer and I stood there for several minutes, reading and touching their headstones, thinking about the life these two people had built together, the children they had brought into the world—four strapping sons, plus two daughters who had died very young, one in infancy, one at age two. And now they were at rest under the Indiana soil, beneath a brilliant blue Indiana sky.

It was an odd feeling, standing so close to John Wooden's parents yet separated from them by the decades. It put everything into perspective. There was a working farm next to the cemetery, and Elmer and I could hear the hubbub of farm activity going on. Looking over the fence, we saw a potbellied pig giving birth right next to the cemetery.

I thought to myself, *In all these years, a lot has changed— yet nothing has changed. It's an internet world, yet farm life is still farm life. The world keeps turning. The old values, the old principles, are still true. They'll always be true.*

That was my introduction to Joshua Hugh Wooden, Coach Wooden's father. At the time, I thought it was the closest I would ever come to this man. But I was wrong.

I couldn't even imagine that, just a few years later, I would have the opportunity to talk to people who actually knew and remembered Joshua Hugh Wooden, the man who wrote the seven-point creed that shaped John Wooden's life.

Thousands of people carry a copy of those seven life principles on a little plastic card in their wallets. Years ago, Coach had them printed up and began handing them out to people, especially young people who needed a guiding hand in their lives.

I've always been fascinated by the unique relationship John Wooden had with his father. I've never seen any other famous person honor his father as John Wooden has honored Joshua Hugh Wooden. Those who know Coach and have worked alongside him make the same observation.

Jay Carty spent three years with John Wooden as a UCLA graduate assistant coach and has also written books with him. Jay told me, "I've always been impressed by the way John Wooden honored the two most important people in his life—his father and his beloved wife, Nell. From what Coach Wooden tells me, his father was firm but gentle. Coach never wanted to let his dad down."

Coach still lives by the seven precepts that his father, Joshua Hugh Wooden, gave him so many years ago. That is quite an amazing legacy for a father to pass down to his son and for that son to bequeath to the world.

My goal in this book is to show you how to apply these seven principles and build them into your daily life. If you memorize this seven-point creed and apply the principles for a lifetime, as John Wooden has done, you can't help but succeed in life.

"Success Is Peace of Mind"

If you are what you eat, then Coach Wooden is made of oatmeal.

He once told me that he and his three brothers—Maurice, Danny, and Billy—ate oatmeal for breakfast almost every morning when they were growing up on the farm near Centerton, Indiana. It seems to me that oatmeal is to John Wooden what spinach is to Popeye—and if all that oatmeal played a part in getting Coach Wooden close to his hundredth birthday, then I want to be made of oatmeal too!

I imagine that the oats Johnny Wooden and his brothers ate every day were grown right there on that Indiana farm. Joshua Hugh Wooden was a hard-working farmer, and though he rarely realized much profit from the crops he grew and the livestock he raised, his family never went hungry, because he raised practically everything they needed to live on.

Coach has described his father as a man who was physically powerful, morally upright, and intellectually curious. He was truly a gentleman, and more than that, he was a *gentle man*. Of his father, Coach Wooden once wrote, "Joshua Hugh Wooden was a farmer—honest, hard-working, and fair. I never heard him speak an unkind word about another person, even on those occasions when he had every reason to. Dad came as close to living the golden rule as anyone I've ever known. He was strong enough to bend a thick iron bar with his bare hands, but he was also a very gentle man who read poetry to his four sons at night. He loved his family deeply."[3]

Joshua Hugh Wooden was a sports enthusiast who encouraged a love of sports in his four boys. He couldn't afford to buy a regulation hoop and basketball for his sons, so he cut the bottom off an old Van Camp tomato basket and put it up inside the barn, nailing it to the hayloft. Johnny's mother stuffed old rags inside a worn-out pair of black cotton hosiery and sewed it up by hand in the approximate shape of a

31

basketball. It wasn't much for dribbling, but it passed, shot, and drained like a regulation basketball.

At night, the four boys slept two to a bed. On cold nights, Joshua Wooden would heat bricks on the wood stove, then wrap towels around the hot bricks and place them under the quilt at the foot of each bed. Only a truly gentle and loving father would take the time to make sure his boys' beds were warm and toasty on a wintry night.

Looking back, John Wooden realized that his parents had a hard life. They never had enough money. They had inherited the little sixty-five-acre farm upon the death of Roxie's father, and it always operated on the razor edge of insolvency. Yet John and his three brothers were never aware that their family went through hard times. In John Wooden's memory, he had an idyllic boyhood. "For my brothers and me," he recalled decades later, "growing up on that little farm in Centerton was almost perfect."[4]

The idyll ended in the late 1920s, while John Wooden was in high school. Joshua became concerned that the farm was not diversified enough. If any of the farm's crops failed, the Wooden family could be in trouble. So as a hedge against crop failure, Joshua Hugh Wooden took out a mortgage on the farm to buy a passel of hogs. To ensure the health of the hogs, he bought a batch of cholera vaccine, but the vaccine was tainted and all the hogs died. That same season, a drought wiped out the crops.

The Wooden family was financially ruined. When Joshua couldn't make the mortgage payments, the bank took everything. It was a hard blow. Not only had Joshua Hugh Wooden lost all he had worked for, but he had also lost his wife's inheritance. Many men would have been bitter. John Wooden recalls that his father never said one word of complaint about his circumstances, never blamed the man who sold him the tainted vaccine, and never expressed any bitterness toward the bank.

Joshua Wooden used those tough times to impress life lessons on his four sons. "Blaming, cursing, hating doesn't help you," he told them. "It hurts you." It was also during this time that he taught his four sons what he called "the two sets of threes": "Never lie, never cheat, never steal," and, "Don't whine, don't complain, don't make excuses."[5]

The family moved into the nearby town of Martinsville, which was famed for its mineral springs. Joshua Hugh Wooden took a job as a masseur, giving massage therapy at the Homelawn Mineral Springs Sanitarium. "I know his spirit was absolutely crushed by what had happened," Coach later recalled, "and his heart ached for what had been lost, yet he lived by the advice he had always given to his sons whenever we fussed about something beyond our control: 'Don't whine, don't complain, don't make excuses. Just do the best you can. Nobody can do more than that.'"[6]

> *Adversity is the state in which man most easily becomes acquainted with himself, being especially free of admirers then.*

Young people are keen observers of their parents' reactions during times of stress, and a teenager named Johnny Wooden was no exception. He recalled that watching his father stick to his principles through hard times "had a most powerful effect on me. That's where I came to see that what you do is more important than what you say you do."[7]

Johnny noticed that his father accepted hardship without blaming or complaining, and his father's example taught young John Wooden a valuable lesson. He wrote, "It was in that lesson, I believe, that my own personal definition of success began to take shape years before I ever wrote it down: 'Success is peace of mind, which is a direct result of self-satisfaction in knowing you made the effort to become the best of which you are capable.'"[8]

Who Was Joshua Wooden?

When Joshua Hugh Wooden moved into Martinsville, he apparently quit going by his first name. When I asked Martinsville old-timers about Joshua Wooden, they didn't know who I was talking about at first. Then they said, "Oh, you mean *Hugh* Wooden?"

One of those Martinsville old-timers was Harry Stultz, who had worked as a bellhop at the Homelawn Mineral Springs Sanitarium. He knew Coach's father well, having worked alongside him for about ten years. "Hugh was one of the nicest people I knew back then," Harry told me. "He had a truly gentle spirit. He was a quiet, straightlaced fellow. After his farm went under, Hugh needed a job to earn money to help educate his four boys. He rented a small apartment in town, and that's where they lived. Hugh's wife worked too, and she was a gentle, quiet lady."

> Things turn out best for the people who make the best of the way things turn out.

I asked Harry what kind of man Hugh Wooden was. "Physically, Hugh was fairly tall and slender," he said. "Working in those hot baths would keep you slender. Hugh would walk to work. It was a seven-block walk from his apartment to the sanitarium. He'd come in at 5:45 in the morning and would work till 4:15 or so most days, six days a week. Then he'd walk home."

What did Hugh Wooden do for enjoyment? "Checkers," said Harry Stultz. "He loved to play checkers. Some days, I'd be waiting for him with a checkerboard, and we'd play checkers for an hour or so until the guests would come down. In all those years, I never did beat him."

I also had the privilege of talking to ninety-two-year-old Harry Johnson of Martinsville. He and his wife, Barbara, have been married for seventy years. Harry worked as a CPA until his retirement in 1989. But retirement hasn't slowed Harry down. He still works every day at his computer in his home office, managing his investments. Harry remembers Coach Wooden's father very well. "Hugh Wooden and I both worked at the Homelawn Mineral Springs Sanitarium during the 1930s and 1940s," he told me. "There were eleven mineral springs sanitariums around town, but Homelawn was the most prestigious. The sanitariums all closed down when the mineral springs went dry around 1967.

"Mineral water has a heavy feel to it, and it smells terrible, like rotten eggs. The water was reported to have healing powers, and, in the old days, some of the quacks would bottle it and sell it, claiming it was good for everything that ails you. But the Homelawn Sanitarium provided honest medical care, according to the medical knowledge at that time.

"Homelawn had about 100 regular employees and up to 150 during the busy season. There were dietitians and medical personnel on duty, including health care experts in many fields. I was a CPA, so I worked in the back office. Hugh Wooden lived about a half mile away and would walk to work like the rest of us. The Woodens lived at 159 South Jefferson in a brick house across from the Carnegie Public Library. The house is still there today.

"Hugh was in charge of the men's bath in the east wing of the sanitarium. He had a staff of workers and had very little contact with the other departments. No one wanted to go back to the baths unless they absolutely had to, because it was very hot and steamy back there. Hugh oversaw the bathtubs, which were huge—as big as battleships. Hugh would work back there practically all day. He'd never leave there. They'd fill these tubs up with mineral water and then keep them at around 90 or 95 degrees. It was stiflingly hot."

As Harry Johnson described the mineral baths, I thought I could hear a shudder in his voice. Even after all those years, it seemed that the heat and steam and sulfur smell of the mineral baths were fresh in his memory. "After the men finished their baths," he said, "they would go for the various kinds of rubs available—salt rubs and so forth. Hugh would do the massages himself or assign his staff. He had five or six clients who tipped him well and requested him every year. The guests at Homelawn came from nearby states—Illinois, Ohio, and Kentucky. Some came from as far away as New York City."

I also heard about the baths from my host, Elmer Reynolds. Though he was too young to have known Hugh Wooden, he had known all four Wooden boys and was well acquainted with Homelawn Mineral Springs Sanitarium. "Around Martinsville," he told me, "we are still proud of long-ago visitors to Homelawn. We had three presidents as guests here: Benjamin Harrison, Grover Cleveland, and Franklin Roosevelt. And Notre Dame football coach Knute Rockne would come to Homelawn, as well as Al Jolson, the singer and movie star. Jolson was a heavy drinker, and he would come to Martinsville to dry out from time to time."

Harry Johnson, the Homelawn CPA, remembered when Joshua Hugh Wooden died. "Mr. Wooden passed away in 1950," he told me. "His four boys all came to my office to get their dad's final paycheck. I remember how big the four of them seemed to me. They filled up my office. That was the last time I saw Johnny Wooden."

I asked Harry what the people of Martinsville thought of Joshua Hugh Wooden. He replied, "Hugh was a fine man, but he wasn't recognized at all in our community. He didn't have a huge impact, and he had very little contact among the town's movers and shakers. I guess you could say he was almost invisible."

Who was Joshua Hugh Wooden? He was a farmer who lost his farm—but never his integrity or his faith in God. He was a hard-working man who would take any job, even working long days in the steaming mineral baths amid the reek of rotten eggs, so that he could earn enough money to send his four sons to college. He was a humble man who lived by the Golden Rule, who never had an unkind word to say about anyone. He was strong yet gentle, a man of the soil and a lover of literature. Above all, he exemplified character, faith, and honor to his sons.

"I never knew Hugh Wooden," Elmer Reynolds told me, "but I have heard about him and thought a lot about him, because of the influence he had on Johnny and his three brothers. Here was a shy, withdrawn man who was never wealthy, famous, or successful in the world's eyes. Yet the wisdom he passed along to his sons is valuable beyond measure and still as relevant today as it was almost a century ago. It's timeless wisdom that never goes out of style, no matter how the world keeps changing. The people who follow Hugh Wooden's wisdom will still be making a positive difference in the world a hundred years from now.

"From everything I've heard, Hugh Wooden was an intelligent man who was reserved and quiet by nature, not because he was uncomfortable around other people but because he was totally comfortable with himself. He wasn't like so many people today who have to be always busy or always talking or always entertained because they can hardly stand their own company. People who knew him say he was comfortable being alone with his thoughts or alone with God.

"Above all, he was a humble man. I think that's where John Wooden learned the quality of humility that marks his life, including his life as a leader and a teacher. You don't usually think of humility as a quality most coaches possess, yet humility is probably the most striking feature of John Wooden's character. I think that may be the key to his success in the sports world. And it all started with his father, who was a role model of humility.

"Joshua Hugh Wooden was a farmer, but when he lost the farm, he didn't hesitate to humble himself and go to work at the local sanitarium. It was a lowly occupation, being a bath attendant. It was unpleasant. I wouldn't call it a menial task, exactly, but neither was it an occupation of great prestige. Johnny's dad had to demonstrate a servantlike attitude every single day, year after year. The example he set shaped the character of his four boys."

Coach John Wooden would certainly agree with Elmer Reynolds's assessment of his father. A few years ago, Coach wrote, "Dad was the best man I ever knew, the one who set the course that guided me through life—what I believe, what I do, and how I do it. In so many ways he made everything happen. And he did it by teaching us in word and deed that the simplest virtues and values were the most important ones."[9]

Who was Joshua Hugh Wooden? He was an absolutely common man—never wealthy, never famous, completely unknown and unheralded. And he was also a leader's leader. He was the leader who led John Wooden, the leader who shaped the life and the values of the greatest coach, the greatest sports leader of all time.

He was a role model for us all.

A Flame in the Soul

There's one more facet of Joshua Hugh Wooden's life that needs to be underscored: He was a *teacher*.

Coach Wooden's father taught him and his brothers a love of literature and poetry, a love of the Bible and prayer, a love of nature and animals, a love of ethics and character, and a simple love of one's fellow human beings. Joshua Hugh

Wooden was very intentional and proactive in the way he taught his sons. He deliberately set aside time for reading good literature and reading the Bible with his family.

As John Wooden later recalled, "There were no athletic scholarships in those days, and Mother and Dad didn't have financial means to help, but all four sons got through college. They worked their way through, and either majored or minored in English, every one of them. Every one became an administrator, all but me. I never became a principal or administrator, but I have a lifetime principal and superintendent's license in the state of Indiana as well as a teacher's license of English."[10] John Wooden once told *Sports Illustrated*, "Oh, I love to teach. I would have been happy being an English teacher my whole life."[11]

> *Learn as if you were to live forever. Live as if you were to die tomorrow.*

Coach Wooden's father inspired a love of learning and a love of teaching in his four sons, and he did so by constantly modeling a love of knowledge. "My father used the immediate to prepare us for the future," Coach once wrote. "That is what effective teachers do—they recognize where you are, and utilize their own knowledge to prepare you for what lies ahead. I don't think it's any coincidence that all four of us boys ended up becoming classroom teachers. A love for learning—whether it was from books or from life—surrounded us from our earliest days, as did a sense of peace that can only stem from true contentedness. These were the lessons my father passed on to his sons."[12]

And just as Joshua Hugh Wooden passed these lessons on to his four sons, his sons have passed these same lessons on to the pupils they have taught. John Wooden has instilled these life lessons into the young players he has coached and mentored over the years. As I have talked to Coach's players, many of whom are now coaches and leaders in their own right, I have been impressed again and again with the fact that so many of them speak appreciatively not only of Coach Wooden but also of Joshua Hugh Wooden, a man they have never met. They have been introduced to this man through Coach Wooden's books and private conversations.

Bill Walton was a star center for John Wooden's unstoppable UCLA Bruins in the early 1970s, winning three consecutive College Player of the Year Awards. He went on to play in the NBA, was inducted into the Basketball Hall of Fame, and (with encouragement from Coach Wooden) overcame a stuttering problem to become a successful sports broadcaster for NBC, ABC, and ESPN.

"Coach Wooden was raised in a different era," Bill told me, "yet his father's seven principles are timeless. Our lives today are so rushed and frenzied that we lose track of these valuable life principles. Joshua Wooden took the time to think through these concepts with a sense of preparation of who he wanted his sons to be. I've heard Coach Wooden talk about the hard times his father went through, and the man must have been overwhelmed by life and by all his responsibilities. Yet he took time to analyze and think through what the foundation of our lives ought to be. He did some original thinking, then distilled his thinking into seven life principles and passed them on to his sons.

"John Wooden's greatness as a coach was not the result of luck or happenstance. He was a great coach and a great human being because his father, Joshua Wooden, had so much foresight and so much insight, and he took the time to teach those values and principles to his sons."

Dave Meyers played forward for Coach Wooden's Bruins and was on the teams that won the NCAA Men's Division I National Championship in 1973 and 1975. Dave has appeared on the cover of *Sports Illustrated* and went on to play for the Milwaukee Bucks. "Coach Wooden lived his dad's seven-point creed," Dave told me. "I don't remember him talking about it to us when I played at UCLA. We were just a bunch of teenagers who wanted to play basketball and become part of the UCLA tradition. I learned about that seven-point creed much later. As I grew older and (I hope) wiser, those principles really began to register with me. I can still hear John Wooden's voice in practice, planting those wisdom principles in our minds. I've been a teacher for many years, and I catch myself teaching my students the same principles Coach taught us."

Keith Erickson was a member of Coach Wooden's 1964 and 1965 NCAA Championship teams. Coach once said that Keith Erickson was the finest athlete he ever coached. Keith told me, "Coach Wooden may have spoken about his father back when we were at UCLA, but none of us was listening. We were focused on playing time, studying, winning games, and girls.

"Over the last ten years, I've gone to visit with Coach more and more, and I've been asking him about the influence of his father. He told me that, at night, his dad would gather the four boys and read to them by candlelight. Joshua Hugh Wooden was not formally educated, but his wisdom came through books and practical life experience. Some of that life experience was very painful. The Wooden family actually had six children, but two daughters died very young. I once heard Coach say, 'Losing those two daughters broke my mother's heart.' Experiences like that teach us things we could never learn from books.

"Coach's father was self-educated, so the seven-point creed came from years of thought and study. There was no Barnes & Noble in Martinsville in 1910. The books of Napoleon Hill, Dale Carnegie, and Zig Zigler hadn't been written yet. But Joshua Wooden spent a lot of time absorbing the wisdom of Solomon and Moses and Jesus. He spent a lot of time thinking about those seven principles that he wanted to pass along to his boys. I can just hear Mr. Wooden say, 'Johnny, if you'll just follow these principles for the rest of your life, you'll do just fine.' We never know when something we say might spark a flame in someone else's soul. That's what those seven principles did in Coach Wooden's soul.

"One day I was visiting Coach's condo, and I noticed a picture of his mother and father on the wall of his den. That prompted me to ask him, 'Coach, how would you like to be remembered at the end of your life?' Without a moment's hesitation, he said, 'I would like to be remembered as a man who came as close as possible to being like my father.' Coach has always viewed his father as being above all men."

Coach Wooden himself wrote of his father, "He had many misfortunes in regard to material things; but he never complained nor compared himself with those who seemed to be more fortunate. In my opinion he came as close to living the philosophy of The Golden Rule as any person that I have ever known. I attribute my emotional balance, which I feel is critical to playing and coaching success, to my father."[13]

One of the greatest privileges of my life has been the honor of knowing Coach Wooden in a personal way—of being invited into his home, sharing meals with him, and drawing from the deep well of his wisdom. He is truly one of the most admirable human beings I have ever known. Like so many people who have met Coach Wooden, I want more of the traits he has. And those traits were instilled in him by a man whom history has largely hidden from view: Joshua Hugh Wooden.

In the next seven chapters, we will explore the seven life principles Coach John Wooden has carried in his wallet throughout his life. These are the principles that shaped his life. These are the principles that are changing my life even now.

Turn the page, my friend. They are about to change yours.

2

Be True to Yourself

From 1966 to 1969, Coach Wooden's UCLA Bruins were anchored by a seven-foot-two-inch African-American named Lew Alcindor, later known as Kareem Abdul-Jabbar. On one occasion, during a road trip, the Bruins' team bus pulled in at a restaurant. As Lew Alcindor sat next to Coach Wooden, looking over the menu, he heard someone a few tables away whisper loudly, "Look at that black freak!"

Coach Wooden saw that his star player was wounded to tears by the comment. "Lewis," he said, "people hate what they don't know—and what they are afraid of. But don't ever stop being yourself."

Alcindor (who would later score a record-setting 38,387 points in a two-decade-long NBA career) grinned back at Coach Wooden. He never forgot that advice.[1]

Joshua Hugh Wooden's first life principle is this: Be true to yourself. In Coach's own commentary on his father's seven-point creed, he wrote, "I believe it is the first point in Dad's creed for a reason. You must know who you are and be true to who you are if you are going to be who you can and should become.

"You must have the courage to be true to yourself."[2]

Joshua and Polonius

I am no authority on Shakespeare, but Coach Wooden is. His father raised him on Shakespeare. When Coach majored in English at Purdue, he studied under Professor Mark Harvey Liddell, an international authority on Shakespeare. Professor Liddell spent an entire semester on *Hamlet* alone. When Coach Wooden began his teaching career at Dayton High School in Kentucky, he also taught Shakespeare. He cites as inspiration for his dad's first life principle a passage from *Hamlet*, the fatherly advice of Polonius to his son Laertes:

> This above all: to thine own self be true,
> And it must follow, as the night the day,
> Thou canst not then be false to any man.[3]

These three lines come at the end of a longer passage in which Polonius gives his son Laertes a series of bullet points of fatherly advice before sending his young son out into the world. Polonius offers this advice in an attempt to prepare his son for the challenges ahead. Perhaps Joshua Wooden thought of this scene from *Hamlet* as he handed his son Johnny a two-dollar bill and a piece of paper containing his seven life principles.

The advice of Joshua Wooden to his son Johnny echoes this scene from *Hamlet* in several ways. In Shakespeare's play, Polonius tells Laertes, "Those friends thou hast, and their adoption tried, / Grapple them to thy soul with hoops of steel."[4] (And no, the phrase "hoops of steel" is not a Shakespearean reference to the game of basketball!) Polonius is, in effect, telling Laertes, "Make friendship a fine art." When you find a good friend and your friendship has withstood the test of time, then hold your friend closely; bind him to your heart with bonds that are as strong as steel.

When Polonius tells Laertes, "Neither a borrower nor a lender be; / For loan oft loses both itself and friend,"[5] he is touching on the same ground as Joshua Hugh Wooden when he says, "Build a shelter against a rainy day." Both fathers are telling their sons to keep the future in mind as they live their lives and manage their resources.

And when Joshua Wooden told his son, "Be true to yourself," he echoed the words of Polonius to Laertes, "To thine own self be true." If you are true to yourself, Polonius adds, then it logically follows that you will never be false to any other person. Faithfulness to others begins with faithfulness to yourself.

What does it mean to be true to yourself? This is not a command to be selfish or self-absorbed. It's a command to be faithful to your highest self, to your values, your honor, your integrity, the reputation you wish to maintain. Be faithful to your commitment to be a person of character, courage, commitment, devotion, perseverance, and diligence. Refuse to compromise yourself. Never sacrifice your principles. Refuse to betray your values. If you remain true to the best that is within you, you will never be false or disloyal to any other person.

Frank Arnold was an assistant to Coach Wooden from 1971 to 1975 and has been a friend of Coach ever since. "To be true to yourself means having integrity," Frank told me. "It means doing the right thing even when no one is looking. Coach believed and lived that principle. Long before I ever met Coach, I had a lesson in this principle that has stuck with me ever since. In 1954, my sophomore year at Idaho State College, we had a three-hour calculus exam. The professor came into the classroom and handed out the test. Then he wrote on the blackboard, 'Do the right thing when no one is looking.' Then he left the room. He trusted every person in that room to have the character to take the test honestly.

"That lesson stuck with me my whole life. Years later, when I met Coach Wooden and he taught those same values, everything Coach said made sense, because I had seen what it looks like when a teacher empowers you to be true to yourself."

> *It isn't what you do but how you do it.*

Another aspect of being true to yourself is being honest with yourself. We human beings have an enormous capacity for self-deception. Former UCLA center Swen Nater (who played under Coach Wooden from 1971 to 1973) told me that Coach always taught his players to be brutally honest with themselves at all times. He explained, "You can fool anyone, but you should never fool yourself. As soon as you fool yourself, you are done."

You can sense a common dynamic in these two scenes—Polonius counseling Laertes and Joshua Wooden counseling his son Johnny. In both cases, you have a father who loves his son, who has done everything possible to raise his son correctly, to teach him right from wrong. In both cases, the father seems reluctant to send his son out alone into the world without a few final words of wisdom to guide him along the way. It's hard for these fathers to let go of their sons, yet they *must* let go.

So the final word of Polonius—and the first word of Joshua Wooden—is, "Be true to yourself." Be alert to the danger of self-deception. Be alert to the impulses and temptations that would undermine your character and destroy your reputation. If you are tempted by alcohol or drugs or pornography or the temptation to cut ethical corners, *don't do it*. Don't deceive yourself into thinking it won't harm you. Don't compromise your integrity. Don't put your reputation at risk. Be true to your highest values and principles, and you will never be false to anyone else.

When I think of the advice of Joshua Wooden to his son Johnny, or the advice of Polonius to his son Laertes, I'm reminded of the fatherly advice we find throughout the biblical book of Proverbs. Here again, we see a father—wise old King Solomon—giving a set of bullet-point guidelines to his son in order to improve the young man's character and his chances of surviving the risks and temptations of a hostile world. For example, in Proverbs 7, Solomon wrote:

> My son, keep my words
>   and store up my commands within you.
> Keep my commands and you will live;
>   guard my teachings as the apple of your eye.
> Bind them on your fingers;
>   write them on the tablet of your heart.
> Say to wisdom, "You are my sister,"
>   and call understanding your kinsman;
> they will keep you from the adulteress,
>   from the wayward wife with her seductive words.
>
> verses 1–5 NIV

Here we see an emotional need that all fathers seem to share: the need to impart wisdom to their sons before sending them out in the world; the need to impress upon their sons the wisdom and knowledge they themselves have acquired at a high price in the school of hard knocks; the need to demonstrate fatherly love—but without getting mushy about it. Every father has known that need. Every father does all he can do for his son but wishes he could do more.

Be Yourself

Dale Brown, longtime basketball coach at LSU, a close friend of Coach Wooden's, and a true John Wooden disciple, told

47

me this story. As Coach Wooden was well into his nineties, his son, Jim, and daughter, Nan, became worried about him living alone in his Encino, California, condominium. So they got him an emergency services pendant to wear around his neck so he could press a button and signal for help if he ever needed it.

One night, he took a fall getting out of bed and broke his collarbone and his wrist. He ended up on the floor, unable to move. A caregiver discovered him in that position the next morning. It was a scary scene. Though he was wearing his pendant, he had deliberately chosen not to use it. The caregiver called for an ambulance, and minutes later he was rushed to the hospital and treated for his injuries.

When his daughter arrived at the hospital, she found him sitting up in bed. "Daddy!" she scolded. "You always talk about character and keeping your word! You promised me you'd wear that emergency pendant! You didn't live up to that! I'm so disappointed in you for breaking your promise!"

Coach hung his head and made no attempt to interrupt Nan as she gave him a tongue-lashing. When she finished, Coach grinned impishly at her and said, "Nan, I promised I'd *wear* it. I didn't promise I'd *use* it."

You may wonder why Coach refused to press the button for help. I wondered the same thing myself, and then it hit me: Coach is fiercely competitive. He had taken a fall, and he was determined to get up under his own power. He would rather spend the night on the floor than press the button and admit defeat.

As Bill Bennett, longtime UCLA sports information director, said, "People think that this kindly, elderly man is everybody's grandpa. But don't you ever forget, as a player and a coach, this man was a savage competitor who hated to lose!" He refused to press that button because he refused to be beaten. That stubborn determination, so uniquely

Woodenesque, is what makes John Wooden who he is and truly exemplifies what it means to be true to yourself.

One aspect of being true to yourself is to *be yourself*. In other words, be the person you were born to be. Brad Holland played for the Bruins from 1975 to 1979. He was the last player Coach recruited to UCLA before retiring. Though Brad never actually played under Coach Wooden, he is one of Coach's most devoted disciples. I asked Brad about the first principle of Coach Wooden's seven-point creed. He told me, "It means don't pretend to be someone you are not. Be who you are so that your life is not a lie. My wife has hung a sign in our house that says, 'I hope to be the person my dog thinks I am.' Isn't that a great statement? If you've ever owned a dog, you know how they practically idolize their masters. Your

> *Be more concerned with your character than your reputation, because your character is what you really are, while your reputation is merely what others think you are.*

dog doesn't realize how flawed you are as a human being. If we could all live up to that image, the world would be a far better place."

Maggie Dixon was only twenty-eight when she accepted the position of women's basketball coach at the United States Military Academy at West Point. Though she had been an assistant at DePaul University in Chicago for four years, she had never served as a head coach before. She was intimidated by the idea of coaching at Army, an institution with decades of military tradition. She wondered if she would fit in.

So she went to her brother, Jamie Dixon, who coached the men's basketball team at the University of Pittsburgh. "Any advice?" she asked.

"I don't know what to tell you, Maggie," he said, "except just be yourself."

Well, Maggie Dixon knew how to be herself. She had gotten the assistant coaching job at DePaul by arriving on campus unannounced, walking into Alumni Hall, locating Coach Doug Bruno, and saying brashly, "I'm Maggie Dixon. Will you hire me?"

So Maggie took her brother's advice and met the challenge head-on, approaching the job at West Point with an air of absolute confidence. "Her bold attitude," said her brother, "tells you everything you want to know about Maggie Dixon."

She led her women's basketball team through the 2005–6 season with a strong 20–10 record. The Army Black Knights had their biggest game against Holy Cross in the Patriot League tournament final. In the closing minutes of a very close game, Maggie took a bold risk, sending in a sophomore forward who had gotten very little playing time all season. "I believe in you so much," Maggie told Stefanie Stone. "Take a deep breath, and have fun."

Stefanie Stone went into the game, and Holy Cross fouled her with eight seconds left to play. The game was tied 68–68 as Stone went to the free-throw line. She missed her first shot. Stone looked at her coach, and Maggie nodded confidently. Stone put up the second shot, and it was good.

Army won by a single point and clinched the Patriot League conference. Next stop, the NCAA tournament.

The Black Knights suffered a painful loss to Tennessee in the first round of that tournament, but just getting to the Big Dance was quite an achievement. It was the first time any Army basketball team, men's or women's, had ever played in the NCAA tournament. After the game, Maggie Dixon returned home to prepare for the next season.

Tragically, however, there would be no next season.

On April 5, 2006, Maggie was in the home of a friend, sharing tea, when she collapsed and lost consciousness. An ambulance took her to Westchester Medical Center in Valhalla, New York. Maggie Dixon never regained consciousness, and she died the following night. An autopsy revealed that Maggie Dixon had an enlarged heart which had never been diagnosed. Though she was a civilian who had served only one year at West Point, Maggie Dixon received a unique Academy honor: burial at West Point Cemetery.[6]

The Women's Basketball Coaches Association now honors outstanding rookie coaches with the annual Maggie Dixon Award. It's quite a tribute to this young coach who took her brother's advice and packed a lifetime of leadership into a single season by simply being herself.

Be the Best You Can Be

Next, to be true to yourself, you must be the best you can be. Coach Wooden once wrote, "In those early days, Dad's message about basketball—and life—was this: 'Johnny, don't try to be better than somebody else, but never cease trying to be the best *you* can be. You have control over that. The other you don't.' It was simple advice: work hard, very hard, at those things I can control and don't lose sleep over the rest of it."[7]

> *Discipline yourself and others won't need to.*

To be the best, you've got to be self-controlled and self-disciplined. "If you are not maintaining self-control," Dave Myers told me, "then you are not being true to yourself. You are letting your circumstances or your emotions or the actions of other people control you. To be true to yourself, you have to be in control of yourself. When I played for Coach Wooden, he used to tell the team, 'If you can't control yourself, others will do it for you. And if you're not controlling yourself, you're not helping the team.'"

Ralph Drollinger played on the great UCLA basketball teams of the early 1970s. He later went into full-time Christian ministry. "Coach always insisted that we concentrate on our own behavior," he told me, "because that's what we can control. He didn't want us to focus on what the other team might do. He almost never showed us any scouting reports on our opponents. We needed to be ourselves and play our game. If we did that, we would control the game. That's what he taught us, and it worked out just as he said."

If you are going to be true to yourself, you must invest in the development and improvement of your own character. Bill Walton told me, "With Coach John Wooden, character development was always number one. And when it came to character, Coach always led by example. The message of his life was, 'If you take time to develop your character, then when the tests of life come, you'll do all right.'"

Dustin Kerns is an assistant coach at Santa Clara University. He told me, "Coach Wooden gave me the seven-point creed, and I carry it in my wallet every day. When I think of John Wooden's years at UCLA, I don't think of the ten NCAA titles. I think of the kind of person Coach was. I know this for sure: If players respect their coach as a person who never compromises his values and principles, those players will believe in him as a leader. They'll follow him anywhere."

In 1974, Coach Wooden and his assistant coaches were called to the office of UCLA athletic director J. D. Morgan. "We just received an offer from one of the television networks," Morgan said. "The network has offered UCLA a lot of money if we will play North Carolina State as the opening game of the upcoming season."

Just a few weeks earlier, the N.C. State Wolfpack had stunned the heavily favored UCLA Bruins in the opening round of the Final Four. The network thought that opening the season with a rematch between the two teams would be a ratings sensation. But as Morgan laid out the terms of the offer, there was one big hitch: The game would be scheduled on a Sunday, the day Coach Wooden set aside as a day of rest. Coach and his wife, Nell, never missed a Sunday attending church in Santa Monica. After church, their children and grandchildren usually came over for Sunday dinner. Would Coach be willing to forego his weekly ritual for this opportunity?

Morgan asked the two assistant coaches, Gary Cunningham and Frank Arnold, what they thought of the offer. Both assistants said they would prefer not to play on Sunday but would do what they had to do. But they both knew it wasn't their opinion that really counted. Morgan turned to Coach Wooden for his response. "Well, Coach? What do you think about the offer?"

"J. D.," Coach said gently, "if you want to schedule that game on Sunday afternoon, go right ahead. But I won't be there."

With that, the discussion was over. There would be no Sunday game.

Andy Hill played basketball at UCLA during the glory days of the 1970s. In those days, he was not John Wooden's most coachable player. In fact, Hill clearly remembers the date October 15, 1969, because it was his very first day of practice as an official member of the Bruins varsity basketball team. It was also the day student protesters called for a walkout to protest the Vietnam War.

Describing himself as "young, self-righteous, and exceedingly cocky," Hill later recalled thinking that "as student-athletes, we should stand side-by-side with other students in protesting the war." He talked a friend, John Ecker, into going with him to see Coach Wooden. Their plan was to demand that Coach cancel the first day of practice in support of the antiwar effort. Ecker let Hill do all the talking.

Hill gave an impassioned speech to Coach Wooden, and he actually expected Coach to be persuaded.

But when Hill finished his pitch, Coach Wooden simply responded, "Andy, *you* don't have to come to practice. . . . You don't *ever* have to come to practice. But there is no way that I am calling off practice for this moratorium."

Hill later reflected, "I had spent my whole life dreaming of playing for John Wooden's Bruins, and on my very first day of practice I had completely ticked him off. Not a great career move."[8]

It wasn't the last time Hill and Coach Wooden would butt heads. In fact, their relationship as player and coach was a contentious one. But after a couple of decades, Hill began to look back on his years with Coach Wooden from a different perspective—one of experience and maturity. He came back and visited his former coach in Wooden's Encino condominium. They developed an entirely new friendship on an entirely new basis—a basis of deep mutual respect. They even wrote a book together, *Be Quick—but Don't Hurry*.

I spoke with Andy Hill, and we talked about all he had learned from his many conversations with Coach. Hill told me, "My wife is a psychological therapist and a keen observer of people. One day, we visited John Wooden at his condo. After we left and got in the car, she said, 'I've never met anyone with that kind of positive regard for a parent in such an unconditional manner.'

"What she said is absolutely true. Coach truly honors his father admiringly and unconditionally—and with very good reason. As I reflect on John Wooden's dad working in the heat of the baths, amid all of that steam and discomfort, I can just hear him saying to his son, 'Don't whine, don't complain, don't make excuses.'

"When my teammates and I played at UCLA, we didn't hear Coach talk about his father's creed. If he had talked about the creed, it wouldn't have made any impact on me as a nineteen- or twenty-year-old student athlete. To me, those seven principles would have sounded trite and meaningless. No, Coach never talked about that seven-point creed around us. He didn't need to. He *lived* that creed. He *was* that creed. And because he was, his players got those principles from him without even realizing it. When you truly *live* your creed, you don't have to talk about it.

"Those players who fought with John Wooden the hardest ultimately became his most outspoken advocates. That's because he let them fight. He wasn't intimidated by a player who had his own opinions. Coach was totally secure in who he was.

"And that really brings us to the first point in that seven-point creed: Be true to yourself. John Wooden had his own sense of priorities, and he refused to compromise them. As a result, he was completely comfortable with himself.

"That's not to say that John Wooden was good at looking out for himself. For example, he was not a good negotiator at contract time. In fact, he was a terrible negotiator. He was overworked and underpaid throughout his career. But there was one thing he absolutely would not budge on: Coach insisted that his wife go with him on all the road trips. That clause was part of all his contracts. He was true to himself with regard to his marriage and his children.

"Coach Wooden had a definition of success that began with six words: 'Success is a state of mind.' Those six words say a lot. Most people struggle internally because they are never satisfied. Even people with enormous success, with all the fame and wealth a person could ever want, are often restless and dissatisfied with their lives. The thing that strikes you about John Wooden is that he is always at peace with himself. That is the secret to the magnetism of his personality. If you have that peace, it will unlock so many things in your life."

Sportswriter Rick Reilly points out that Coach Wooden "never made more than $35,000 a year, including 1975, the year he won his 10th national championship, and never asked for a raise."[9] In fact, in the late 1960s, when the Bruins had reached the pinnacle of success, Jack Kent Cooke, owner of the L.A. Lakers, offered Coach *ten times* his UCLA salary to coach the Lakers. Coach said he wasn't interested. "Nobody's worth that kind of money," he replied. "It's not about money."

> *Don't let making a living prevent you from making a life.*

Cooke couldn't believe his ears. He'd never heard *anyone* say it's not about the money. It's *always* about the money! But Coach Wooden went on to explain that he was coaching at UCLA because he didn't want to give up teaching, not at a hundred times his present salary.[10] Coach was determined to remain true to himself.

Be True to Your Potential

Playwright Neil Simon once gave a commencement address with the theme of being true to yourself. He said, "Don't listen to those who say, 'It's not done that way.' Maybe it's not, but maybe you will. Don't listen to those who say, 'You're taking too big a chance.' Michelangelo would have painted the Sistine floor, and it would surely be rubbed out by today. Most importantly, don't listen when the little voice of fear inside of you rears its ugly head and says, 'They're all smarter than you out there. They're more talented, they're taller, blonder, prettier, luckier and have connections. . . .' I firmly believe that if you follow a path that interests you . . . the chances are you'll be a person worthy of your own respect."[11]

Or, as John Wooden himself once put it, "Do not be too concerned about what others may think of you. Be very concerned about what you think of yourself."[12]

To be true to yourself means to be true to your greatest potential. It means fulfilling all of your God-given capacity for doing good works and achieving great things. We are all capable of doing far more than we imagine. Jay Carty, Coach's graduate assistant at UCLA, told me, "Coach's philosophy was never to settle for less than 100 percent. He didn't obsess over wins and losses, but he always wanted you to ask yourself, 'Did I give my maximum effort? Did I do the very best that I was capable of doing? And if not, why not?'"

Coaches often talk about "giving 110 percent." There is no such thing as 110 percent. The most any of us can give is 100 percent. The problem is that most of us *think* we are giving 100 percent when we are actually giving only 95 percent, 90 percent, or even less. We don't know what our true capabilities are. For almost all of us, there are depths of energy, effort, character, talent, and ability that we haven't even begun to tap. That's why coaches talk about "giving 110 percent." They are trying to get you to realize that, even though you *think* you've reached down and summoned everything you've got, there are still untapped resources within you. You can still work harder, persevere longer, and endure more pain than you can imagine.

Don't measure yourself by what you have accomplished but by what you should have accomplished with your ability.

So be true to yourself. Be true to your greatest potential. Reach down, dig deep, and find that extra measure of will and determination to keep reaching for your goals.

Bill Bennett told me, "This seven-point creed comes right back to John Wooden's philosophy of being the best you are capable of being. You must be consistent on a daily basis.

You can't take days off. Be the best you can be day after day, and ultimately you will be the best, period."

Be True to Your Principles

And that brings us to one final test of what it means to be true to yourself: the test of temptation. Ralph Drollinger explained it to me this way: "When you are tempted to compromise your principles (and you will be), you have to be true to yourself and be like Daniel and Joseph in the Bible. They paid a heavy price to stand by their principles and do the right thing day after day. The king decreed that all the people of the nation should worship him as a god or be executed, but Daniel defied the decree, remaining true to his principles. And God rewarded his faithfulness.

"Joseph was tested and tempted when his employer's wife repeatedly tried to seduce him, but Joseph remained true to his principles, even at the cost of being falsely imprisoned. And God rewarded Joseph's faithfulness too. If you remain true to yourself and true to your principles, you can live with yourself during the daytime and sleep with a clear conscience at night."

Another former Bruin who played for Coach Wooden, Jamaal Wilkes, put it this way: "You have to live with your choices. You have to live with your responses to temptation. You have to live with how you treat people. That is all part of being true to yourself."

While this book was being written, I had a speaking engagement in Orlando. The emcee who introduced me was Dick Bunce, a professor at Virginia Commonwealth University in Richmond. He shared with me a personal story over lunch—a story Coach Wooden would certainly appreciate. "When I was fifteen," Dick told me, "I decided it was time for me to start shaving. That would be the mark of manhood for me—even though I had only one hair on my face. I kept bugging my dad to teach me how to shave.

"Finally, he relented and took me to the bathroom sink. He took down a straight-edged razor and the leather strop he used to sharpen it. He showed me how to lather up my face, then he said, 'One more thing, Dick. It's a lot easier to shave in the morning if you don't mind looking at the face in the mirror.'

"Then he walked out, leaving me in a state of confusion. I didn't understand what he meant that day—but I understand now. My dad lived to be eighty-one years old. The advice he gave me when he taught me to shave was the most important life lesson he ever gave me."

Deep Down, We Know

When John Wooden attended Purdue University, he played guard for the Boilermakers, coached by the legendary Ward "Piggy" Lambert. There he led Purdue to the 1932 National Championship and was named All–Big Ten, All-Midwestern, and three-time All-American. He was nicknamed "The Indiana Rubber Man" because, as he explained, "I always bounced off the floor if I went down."

In 1932, the year he graduated from Purdue with an English degree, a professional basketball team offered him $5,000 to join a barnstorming tour across the country. In those days, $5,000 was a lot of money. He had already been offered a job teaching and coaching at Indiana Teacher's College (now known as Indiana State University), a job that paid $1,500 a year for teaching five English classes per day and coaching four sports. That $5,000-a-year pro basketball gig looked mighty tempting.

So John Wooden went to Coach Lambert for advice. The coach listened patiently as his star player described his options. Then Lambert said, "That's a lot of money, isn't it, John?"

"Yes, sir. It's a lot of money."

"Is that what you came to Purdue for?"

"Sir?"

"I mean, did you come here to Purdue University so that you could travel the country and play professional basketball?"

John Wooden cleared his throat. "Um, no sir. I came here to get an education. And I got an education, sir. A very good one."

"Well, then, John, maybe you should use it. But you'll have to decide that for yourself."

Coach Lambert left the decision to John Wooden, but the way he framed the decision made the choice very clear. Wooden could make $5,000 a year as a barnstorming basketball player, or he could make $1,500 a year as an educator, putting his university training to good use.

John Wooden later recalled, "Coach Lambert . . . had gotten me back to Dad's first creed: Be true to yourself.

"Deep down I had known what the correct decision was. Coach Lambert just helped bring it out. I really wanted to teach and coach."[13]

Deep down, we almost always know what we should do at the key decision points in our lives. As General Norman Schwarzkopf once said, "The truth of the matter is that you always know the right thing to do. The hard part is doing it."[14]

We may say, "I'm confused. I don't know what to do." But that's seldom true. We know *exactly* what we should do, but we don't want to do it. So we look for an escape hatch, a back door, a way out. We go to our friends and ask for their advice, hoping they will give us the answer we want to hear, not the answer we *know* to be true.

John Wooden was fortunate to have a coach who asked the right questions and reminded him of his father's first principle in his seven-point creed: Be true to yourself. What is the tough decision you're facing right now? No one can make that decision for you. In fact, I think you already know the answer.

Be true to yourself—to your highest self, your values, your character, your honor, and your integrity. Be true to yourself, and you'll never be false to anyone else.

3

Help Others

In 1964, Coach Wooden was honored with his first of seven NCAA College Basketball's Coach of the Year awards, and he took his Bruins to the Final Four. At the hotel where he stayed for the tournament, he was crossing the lobby when he heard someone call out, "Coach Wooden!"

He turned, and two men approached, introducing themselves as Coach Scotty Robertson of Louisiana Tech and his assistant, Don Landry. "We're sorry to impose," Robertson said, "but we were wondering if you could spare a few minutes to help us with a problem."

Coach Wooden agreed, and they found some chairs and sat down. Coach Robertson proceeded to explain: For years, Tech had been an undersized team using a run-and-gun approach. But the school had recently recruited three seven-footers, and the team needed a new coaching strategy. "Coach Wooden," Robertson said, "we know you've had a lot of experience coaching seven-foot players. What kinds of adjustments should we make?"

For the next ninety minutes, Coach Wooden gave the two men a free clinic on big-man strategy. There aren't many people who would give so generously of their time to help a potential opponent, but that's the kind of man Coach Wooden is.

Dale Brown told me, "I always end my coaching clinics by telling of the day I visited John Wooden at his home in Los Angeles when I was a very young coach. At the end of our visit, Coach Wooden and his wife, Nell, walked me to my car. John put his arm around me and said, 'Dale, I really enjoyed spending time with you. But I could have saved you a lot of time if I had just told you my secrets of coaching.'

"I practically broke my neck reaching for my pen and pad so I could scribble down those nuggets of Coach's wisdom. I thought, *This is really going to do it for me!*

"Coach said, 'One, make sure you always have better players than the team you play. Two, make sure that your players put the team above themselves. Three—and this is a very important point—always practice simplicity with constant repetition, and you will be successful.'" Dale Brown never forgot that advice, and he never forgot Coach Wooden's kindness.

You have not lived a perfect day until you've done something for somebody who cannot repay you.

Ed Ehlers played basketball for Coach Wooden at Indiana State in the late 1940s before going on to play professionally in the NBA and the NFL. While at State, Ehlers repeatedly had his nose broken in games, and those injuries caused him to suffer chronic breathing problems. One day, a doctor came to Ehlers's home and told him he would perform an operation that would improve his breathing. Ehlers asked the doctor who had sent him. The doctor refused to say. Then Ehlers asked how much the operation would cost. The doctor said, "It won't cost *you* anything. It's all been taken care of."

So Ed Ehlers had his operation at no cost to him. No one ever *officially* told Ehlers who arranged for the surgery. But in telling the story years later, Ehlers said there was only one person who could have done it. "Coach Wooden was always helping somebody," he said.

As Coach himself once wrote, "You cannot have a perfect day without helping others with no thought of getting something in return. . . . The basic precept of all the great religions is the Golden Rule: Do unto others as you would have them do unto you. Simply stated, it means, 'Help others.'"[1]

An Example of Helping

My friend and fellow Wake Forest alum Gil McGregor, longtime broadcaster for the Charlotte (now New Orleans) Hornets, told me, "A group in Winston-Salem attempted to contact Dr. Maya Angelou, hoping she would agree to cook dinner as a fund-raiser for the March of Dimes. When they were unable to reach her, someone in the group called me and said, 'I hear you know Dr. Angelou personally. Would you be able to help us get in touch with her?' So I called her and asked if she would be willing to help the cause. She immediately said yes. I thanked her, then added, 'Dr. Angelou, I hope you don't feel I'm using our friendship in order to get you to volunteer.' She laughed and said, 'Mr. McGregor, if one cannot be used, it only means that one is useless.'"

Dale Brown told me a story that a friend shared with him. "When my dad got out of high school," Dale's friend said, "he and a buddy hitchhiked from Spokane to Yellowstone National Park. When the two hitchhikers got to the entrance of Yellowstone, a nice man and his wife picked them up on the side of the road. The man and his wife drove them through the park, shared their food with them, and gave them a place to stay. That gracious couple was John and Nell Wooden."

Gail Goodrich Jr. played for Coach Wooden when the Bruins won their first two national championships in 1964 and 1965. He went on to play for the Los Angeles Lakers and was the team's top scorer during the Lakers' thirty-three-game winning streak in 1971–72. "When I was at UCLA," he told me, "we played in Arnold Gym on campus. At that time, scholarship players had to do 250 hours a year of work. Every day before practice we had to sweep the gymnasium floor. Every day, John Wooden was out there helping with the sweeping."

Former UCLA forward Jamaal Wilkes told me, "'Help others'—that principle really sums up John Wooden's life. His example has impacted me greatly. When you help others, you don't do it expecting anything in return. You just help people because it's the right thing to do. Yet it always seems to work out that when you help other people, you help yourself as well."

And Coach Wooden's former UCLA assistant Denny Crum said, "John Wooden is my role model. I've seen how Coach lived his life to make others' lives better, and I've done my best to emulate him."

Tom Wasdin was head basketball coach at Jacksonville University in the early 1970s and now heads Wasdin Associates, a commercial and residential real estate company in Florida. He told me, "I was a high school coach when I attended a coaching clinic at Stetson University where Coach Wooden was one of the keynote speakers. That was the summer after he won his first national championship. Following his speech, I went up and introduced myself. Even though I was only a high school coach, he treated me with great respect and made me feel that he was sincerely interested in helping me with my chosen career."

Until the years finally caught up with him, Coach Wooden was remarkably accessible to the public. All you had to do was get up early in the morning and show up for breakfast at VIP'S Restaurant on Ventura Boulevard in Tarzana, California. You could find him there almost every morning. He never needed a menu. He just ordered his usual Number 4 Special. There were always friends there having breakfast with him—some old friends going back to his UCLA days, and some new friends who just wanted to learn from him and absorb some of his wisdom. Long after Coach Wooden retired from the game, a lot of people came to VIP'S to be coached and mentored by him.

One of those who often ate breakfast with Coach was his former UCLA graduate assistant Jay Carty, who told me, "It was fascinating to watch Coach at VIP'S. He'd visit all the different tables and just let the people siphon off wisdom from him."

Two of Coach Wooden's greatest heroes (besides his father) were Abraham Lincoln and Mother Teresa. Bill Walton shared this insight with me: "Coach learned from Mother Teresa about a selfless nature, about the importance of helping others. John Wooden's teams played that way. He wouldn't allow one guy to do all the dribbling while four others stood around watching. Our job was to set someone else up for the shot—to inspire and persevere in order to help lift up everyone on the team so that we could all make our dreams come true.

"In my family, my wife and I made sure we taught the importance of helping others. Our four sons are all doing well in life and are all extremely happy for each other's successes. Greed and selfishness can ruin the success of a family or a team. I learned the team game as a youngster in San Diego long before I went to UCLA. All my youth coaches taught the way John Wooden does, because they were all John Wooden disciples."

Can basketball players actually improve their game by learning from Mother Teresa? Absolutely. The character traits that produce an admirable human being also make better teams and better players—and that is especially true of the character trait of helping others. In fact, the game of basketball is intentionally designed to favor the team that is the least selfish and the most focused on helping others. It is a game in which players actually improve their statistics by making an assist.

Coach Wooden underscored the value of the assist by teaching his players to share credit for every shot. He once said, "If a player scored off a pass, I wanted him to point to the man giving the assist until they made eye contact in a gesture of thanks and acknowledgement. I started that with my high school teams. I also wanted a gesture of thanks done for a good pickup, for help on defense or for any other good play."[2]

Retired University of North Carolina basketball coach Dean Smith said that when he heard about Coach Wooden's point-for-the-assist rule, he instituted it at Chapel Hill. "We even had the Bobby Jones Rule," he said, speaking of an enhancement to Coach Wooden's point rule. During a game in the 1970s, Smith said, "Bobby missed a layup after a beautiful pass from George Karl. Bobby still pointed to him. To this day, the Carolina players point to the passer even after a missed layup."[3]

Helping the Next Generation

While I lived in Bloomington from 1962 to 1964, I met a woman known as Mom Burgher. She and her husband, Bob, owned Burgher's Grill on Main Street in the center of Bloomington. Burgher's Grill was one of those classic American eateries that you hardly ever see anymore in this fast-food franchise world. Their burgers were the best I've ever had—and Bob and Mom Burgher were two of the best people I've ever known. Like Joshua Wooden and his son John, they were dedicated to helping others.

During the lunch-hour rush, they were busy grilling and serving up burgers and fries, but once the rush was over, Mom would come out from behind the counter, stop by your booth, and chat with you. She didn't just talk about the weather. She was genuinely interested in the people who passed through her eatery, most of whom were students from the university. She wanted to know all about your plans and dreams for the future. Maybe that's how she came to be called Mom—her interest in young people was so sincere and motherly.

I was a guest in the Burghers' home many times, and I can still picture its walls covered with framed photos of "Mom's boys," pictures sent to her over the years by students after they had left Indiana University. There were wedding pictures, family pictures, pictures of young men in military uniforms. Mom Burgher had no children of her own, but she had many sons—and I was one of them. She called all the athletes, coaches, and students at Indiana University "my boys." We all knew we could knock on her door at any time of the day or night, and she'd let us in, serve up a piece of fresh apple pie, and let us talk about whatever was bothering us.

Mom Burgher attended all the Hoosier football and basketball games, decked out in cream and crimson. She was our friend, our counselor, and yes, she was Mom. Many times, I went to her house, and she helped me work through some problem in my academic or personal life. Long after Bob Burgher passed away, Mom continued to mentor the students who passed through Bloomington.

I exchanged notes and cards with Mom long after I left. Whenever I passed through Indiana, I went out of my way to stop by Mom's for a visit. When she passed away in her eighties, she left a legacy of helping literally hundreds of people, including a young Pat Williams. I once assumed that every college town must have a Mom Burgher, but in later years I came to realize that people like her are actually quite rare. The world needs more caring people like Mom Burgher, people who are willing to open their homes and live a lifestyle of helping other people.

Mom Burgher had a lot in common with Coach Wooden. Both Mom and Coach were focused on influencing young lives. After Coach retired, someone asked him what he missed most about coaching. His reply: "The practices. Not the rings or the titles. I'm a teacher, and I miss teaching the young men."

Bill Walton agreed with Coach's description of himself as a teacher, first and foremost. "Above all, John Wooden was a teacher," Walton said. "He taught life, not basketball. The way he taught us how to learn changed my life."[4]

Dale Murphy is a retired Major League Baseball first baseman and outfielder best remembered for his long career with the Atlanta Braves. He won two consecutive National League MVP awards, four consecutive Silver Slugger awards, and five consecutive Gold Glove awards. But what really sets Dale Murphy apart is the example he sets for young people.

In the late 1980s, as his career began to wane, Murphy saw that something new was making its way into the league: steroids. He knew that some players were using steroids to extend their playing careers, but he was not willing to cheat just to get a few more years in the game. He was intensely aware of his influence on young people, and he didn't want to do anything that might disappoint or disillusion his young fans.

Throughout his career, Murphy was known as a player of good habits and clean living. He didn't drink, smoke, endorse unwholesome products, or allow himself to be photographed in the embrace of a woman. He kept his language clean. His favorite movie is *It's a Wonderful Life* starring Jimmy Stewart and Donna Reed. He once turned down $25,000 in automobile endorsement money because he test-drove the car and said he couldn't endorse it with a clear conscience. He has donated untold hours to help the American Heart Association, the March of Dimes, and the Make-a-Wish Foundation.

One of the most emotionally compelling moments of Murphy's career came in June 1983, before a Braves home game against San Francisco. He received word that six-year-old accident victim Elizabeth Smith was in the stands, wanting to see him hit a home run. The girl had lost both hands and one leg several months earlier when she had stepped on a downed power line. Murphy went up in the stands and gave the girl some souvenirs. Then Elizabeth's nurse asked him, "Mr. Murphy, could you please hit a home run for Elizabeth?"

The little girl looked up at him in awe. How could he guarantee a home run, but how could he say no? "Well," he said, "okay."

He took the field, and before the game was over, he had hit not one but *two* homers, driving in all three Atlanta runs. The Braves beat the Giants 3–2.

As a player and since his retirement, Dale Murphy has campaigned against drug abuse in sports. His biggest concern is the influence that drug-abusing athletes have on the next generation. He has no tolerance for drug use in sports and believes there should be zero tolerance in the leagues. "The guys using this stuff are messing with the integrity of the game," he says. "I'm tired of this. Let's kick them out."

As part of his own personal war against drug abuse, Murphy founded the I Won't Cheat Foundation (www.iwontcheat. com). He wants to encourage young people to stay away from mind-altering and performance-enhancing drugs. His website presents the medical facts about steroids, and young people can sign an online pledge "not to cheat in sports, in the classroom, or in life."

Dale Murphy is an athlete who uses his position to help young people. He doesn't just *preach* clean living. He *practices* what he preaches—always has, always will. This world needs more people like Dale Murphy—and like Coach Wooden.[5]

One of the most important things Coach has done to help the next generation is his invention of the pyramid of success, his famed pyramid-shaped diagram for success in basketball and in life. The pyramid consists of five rows of building blocks, each row building on the row below. These building blocks consist of such character qualities as industriousness, friendship, loyalty, cooperation, enthusiasm, self-control, and so forth, building toward competitive greatness at the apex.

The pyramid of success has been such a powerful success concept that Coach has been hired by corporations to give lectures on it. Some of the lecture fees he has received for a single speech on the pyramid have exceeded his entire coaching salary for a single year, yet Coach Wooden typically invests those fees in education funds for his grandchildren and great-grandchildren.

He has given autographed copies of his *Pyramid of Success* book to literally tens of thousands of young people at basketball camps and other events over the years. As a result, generations of young people have grown up reciting Coach Wooden's unique formulation of what it means to have a successful life: "Success is peace of mind, which is a direct result of self-satisfaction in knowing you made the effort to become the best of which you are capable."

"As a Christian and a teacher," Frank Arnold told me, "Coach Wooden views helping others as his life's calling. He believes he was born to influence and serve young people. That's why Coach has such purpose and meaning in his life. He fulfills his calling every single day.

"In the spring of 2010, when coach was ninety-nine and a half years old, the twelve-year-old son of a friend of mine had a school assignment. He had to interview somebody of note. So I helped set up a meeting so the boy could interview

Coach. They met at VIP'S, and Coach was in his wheelchair. The boy was scared to death!

"They were eating breakfast, and the boy had his tape recorder. He was all ready to go and had his questions ready. Then Coach said, 'Now, son, come over here and sit with me.' The boy sidled over a little closer. Coach reached out from his wheelchair and said, 'You're not close enough. You need to get closer.' Then he proceeded to do the interview with the young man.

"As this went on, the restaurant began to fill with people, and they all wanted Coach to sign autographs. And he did. After a while, I could see that he was getting too tired to sign his name anymore. So I had to intercede and get Coach out of there, because he would not have stopped.

"One more thing—the boy got an A+ on his paper."

Givers and Takers

Bill Bennett, UCLA sports information director, told me, "John Wooden's father set the standard for helping others and treating people fairly. He was a role model and example to his sons because he lived what he preached. Every day, John Wooden saw his father stand up for what he believed.

"I was in a store recently and saw a poster on the wall with a quote from Mother Teresa, one of John Wooden's heroes. It said, 'The three most important things in life are Be kind . . . Be kind . . . Be kind.' That's Coach's outlook on life in a nutshell."

You never know where you'll find people living out the adage "Be kind." Sometimes there's serious caring and helping going on behind a cheerleader's pom-poms. Suzanne Mitchell was the director of the Dallas Cowboys cheerleader squad from 1976 to 1989. A few years ago, she talked to *Newsweek* about how most people think of the Cowboys' cheerleaders as nothing more than a sideshow for football fans who like "a little sex with their violence." Critics of the cheerleader squad would write to her and accuse her of debasing women on national TV.

Mitchell would write back: "What were you doing last Christmas Eve? My girls were sitting at midnight in a flight shack on the DMZ in Korea after having entertained more than 5,000 troops, done four shows, visited eight bases. They were asleep at midnight in minus 20 degrees. . . . What's the last thing you did for your country?"

Her critics would usually respond, "I'm sorry. I didn't know."[6]

If you are as old as I am, you may recall Danny Thomas as the star of the classic TV sitcom *Make Room for Daddy*. He was also the founder of St. Jude Children's Hospital in Memphis, a world-famous research and treatment center for childhood diseases, especially cancer. St. Jude's began with a prayer.

In 1943, Danny Thomas was barely surviving, caring for a pregnant wife while earning five dollars a week as a singer-comedian in small nightclubs. His uncle urged him to give up show business and work for him in the family butcher shop. A devout Catholic, Thomas went to St. Jude's Church and prayed, "Show me my way in life, and I will build you a shrine."

His prayer was answered a short time later when he got a booking at Chez Paris in Chicago. Audiences loved him, and his booking was extended week after week—for five years. His nightclub popularity got him acting roles in films and on television. He never forgot his promise to God. He went to a Catholic cardinal, explained the promise he had made in prayer, and asked what sort of shrine would be suitable. The cardinal told him, "This world has plenty of statues but not enough hospitals for children who are sick." And that's how St. Jude Children's Hospital was born.

Thomas began raising funds and recruiting staff for the hospital in 1957. The task of building the hospital would take five years.

In 1959, while Thomas was crisscrossing the country, raising funds to build his hospital, he visited Peoria State Hospital in Illinois to meet with hospital administrators, staff, and supporters. At one point, Thomas stood with members of the staff, posing for publicity stills, when he heard a boy shouting, "Danny Thomas! If you are here, if you're really here, I've got to see you!"

Looking around, Thomas saw an eleven-year-old boy in a wheelchair, blind and trembling from palsy. Abandoned as an infant and blind from birth, the boy was known as Billy Johnson. He held out an envelope.

Thomas knelt by the boy's wheelchair. "I'm here," he said. "I'm Danny Thomas."

Billy pressed the envelope into Thomas's hand. "Take this," the boy said. "There's seventy-five cents in here. I saved my candy money. I want you to use this to build that hospital for the kids."

Weeping openly, Thomas took the envelope and thanked the boy.

He never spent Billy Johnson's seventy-five cents. Instead, he went around the country and spoke to groups of people. He held up Billy's coins in front of the audience and told the story of Billy Johnson's generosity. That story pried open countless checkbooks and pocketbooks. Billy Johnson helped Danny Thomas raise millions of dollars for St. Jude Hospital.

The hospital opened its doors in 1962. At that time, only 4 percent of children with acute lymphocytic leukemia survived. Thanks to research conducted at St. Jude, the survival rate soared to 73 percent by 1991. That's just one of many St. Jude success stories. Today, a statue of St. Jude stands in front of the hospital, and Billy Johnson's seventy-five-cent donation is sealed inside the cornerstone beneath the statute—a fitting shrine to an entertainer and a little boy who were both committed to helping others.[7]

Danny Thomas once said, "All of us are born for a reason, but all of us don't discover why. Success in life has nothing to do with what you've gained in life or accomplished for yourself. It's what you do for others."[8] And his daughter, Marlo Thomas, added, "My father said there were two kinds of people in the world: givers and takers. The takers may eat better, but the givers sleep better."[9]

Living by the Golden Rule

In 1948, John Wooden was head coach of the Indiana State basketball team, which included a player named Clarence Walker. Though Walker wasn't one of the starting five, he was an effective role player who had helped Indiana State win a berth at the National Association of Intercollegiate Athletics (NAIA) tournament in Kansas City. Thirty-two teams were invited, and the last team standing would be the small college national champion.

Unfortunately, the color barrier was still an issue in college sports in 1948. This was only one year after Jackie Robinson broke the color barrier in Major League Baseball. NAIA officials told Coach Wooden that his team was invited—all except Clarence Walker. People of color were not allowed on the floor of the Kansas City Municipal Auditorium.

An appearance in the NAIA tournament would have been a major résumé enhancement for young Coach Wooden, but the conditions were unacceptable. Coach didn't even pause to consider the invitation. "If I can't bring Clarence," he said, "we're not coming."

When the national news media heard that Indiana State had withdrawn from the tournament rather than leave Clarence Walker behind, the story went viral. When the *New York*

Times carried the story, the coach at Manhattan College—the odds-on favorite to win the tournament—made an announcement of his own: If Indiana State could not bring its entire team, Manhattan College would boycott the tournament.

Now NAIA officials had a huge problem: Their biggest draw was backing out of the tournament. There was only one thing to do: let Clarence Walker play. As a result, Walker became the first African-American to play basketball at the Municipal Auditorium in Kansas City. Clarence Walker broke the color barrier in college basketball because Coach Wooden took a stand for his principles—and his players.

> *Consider the rights of others before your own feelings and the feelings of others before your own rights.*

Ensuring that people are treated fairly, even when you have to pay a price to do so, is yet another way of helping people. John Wooden took that stand because that's how his father, Joshua Wooden, had raised him. As Coach Wooden wrote in *They Call Me Coach*, "My dad did love his fellow-man sincerely. He was honest to the nth degree and had a great trust and faith in the Lord. And he taught us many lessons in integrity and honesty which we never forgot."[10]

Coach always seemed astonished and amazed by racism, as if he could not imagine how people could mistreat other people because of the color of their skin. He was horrified by the treatment his star center, Lew Alcindor (Kareem Abdul-Jabbar), often endured. "I learned more from Lewis about man's inhumanity to man," he once wrote, "than from anybody else."[11]

When asked what he is most proud of in his career, Coach Wooden does not talk about championships or winning streaks or records or awards. Instead, he cherishes his reputation as a coach who always treated his players fairly. "What am I proud of?" he wrote. "After we'd won a national championship game, a reporter asked one of my players what kind of racial problems we had on the team. The player looked at the reporter and said, 'You don't know our coach, do you? He doesn't see color, he sees ballplayers.' And he turned and walked away. That's what I'm proud of."[12]

Rightfully so. John Wooden lives his life as his father taught him. He lives by the Golden Rule.

The Dirty Shoulders Principle

Brad Holland told me, "John Wooden loves to give credit to others and never feels he has it all figured out. He's always saying, 'I'm just a man who was provided with great leadership as a youngster by a remarkable father.' His dad took the time to teach young Johnny, and as a result, Coach John Wooden has always had great respect for his dad. I've never heard Coach take any credit for his own accomplishments or his own character. He always deflects the credit away from himself and gives it to God, to his players, and above all, to his father."

Jay Carty recalled, "Coach Wooden was in charge and his word was law, but that didn't mean he wasn't a good listener. He was open to ideas, and he would listen patiently and give you a chance to make your case. I had played against UCLA when I was at Oregon State in the early 1960s. After that, I was in graduate school at UCLA and made my pitch to John Wooden on why Lew Alcindor would be better off working against me in practice than against some player on the second unit. Coach bought my idea and employed me to do that. It worked out quite well.

"Now jump ahead about thirty-five years. I was a minister and had lost my vocal chords. My ministry and my livelihood were in jeopardy. I sat down with Coach Wooden one morning at VIP'S to discuss a book idea. He was already working with another writer on a book, but he saw that I had lost a great deal. He had compassion for me, and he agreed to do a book with me. He did it purely for my sake and not for himself. He did it out of friendship. The book we did was titled *Coach Wooden: One-on-One*. It did well, and the publisher then asked us to write a second book, *Coach Wooden's Pyramid of Success*."

Coach Wooden teaches us to look at helping others as an end in itself, not as a means to an end. Some people help other people as a way of manipulating them: "I helped you, now you owe me." But Coach focuses on helping people who cannot pay him back. He helps others purely for the joy and satisfaction of helping others, expecting nothing in return. If we help other people out of an ulterior and selfish motive, we aren't truly helping others—we're just helping ourselves.

Gil McGregor taught me a concept he calls "The Dirty Shoulders Principle." He told me that, in a figurative sense, all great people have dirty shoulders. People of true greatness are always lifting others up and letting them stand tall on their own shoulders. They don't care who gets the credit. They don't mind if their own shoulders get dirty. They just want to lift other people up.

That's the kind of greatness we continually see in the life of Coach Wooden—and in the life of his father, Joshua Hugh Wooden. These men, father and son, were always helping others. They had a mind-set that said, "Find some dirty windows and wash them. Find a neighbor's lawn and mow it. Clean up the mess, even if you didn't make it. Read to a child. Find some people to help, and *serve* them."

Former UCLA guard Henry Bibby explained it to me this way: "When I played for him, Coach never talked about his dad. He simply stressed the importance of doing the right thing and being a good person. That had to come from his father's beliefs. Coach was a strict disciplinarian and a real rules guy. He wanted discipline and structure on all his teams. That had to come from the solid background he grew up with in Indiana.

"When I was coaching at USC, I was on a recruiting trip in the Midwest. I was able to visit Martinsville and went to John Wooden's old high school. I visited his parents' cemetery site and called Coach while I was there. He gave me a guided tour of the cemetery from his condo in Encino. He had an encyclopedic memory of the cemetery, knew exactly who was buried where, and he told me the things he remembered about each one. That experience gave me a lot of insight into who Coach is and the place that shaped his life and his values.

"Who is Coach Wooden? He's a guy who never sought out the limelight. He was always trying to stay behind the scenes. He never cared about receiving accolades for his coaching; it was all about the team. I'm sure John Wooden learned that character quality from his dad. In a way, I wish I could have known his dad. But in a real sense, I already do. Coach Wooden is his father's son. That says it all."

Coach himself wrote, "My father truly had a love for every living creature, and it was apparent in the way he worked with both animals and people. There was a time when we were working at the local gravel pit and a team of horses was struggling with the load. Their driver was whipping them and hollering and raising a ruckus, but my father stepped up to the team and spoke to them quietly, then grasped the bridle and calmly led them forward. It was an incredible reminder that gentleness can fix in a moment what an hour of shouting fails to achieve."[13]

What a great example of kindness and gentleness Joshua Wooden set for his son! That example helps to explain a story told to me by Andy Hill: "In August 2009, after Coach received the *Sporting News* award as the greatest coach in sports history, I was there with about fourteen other former Bruins at the press conference. Coach spoke to the group, and his closing words to us were, 'I just wish I could have done more for all of you.' All at once, fifteen guys reached for their handkerchiefs."

Helping others: that's the heart and soul of Coach John Wooden. May it also be your heart and soul—and mine.

4

Make Each Day
Your Masterpiece

Writer Don Yeager was Coach Wooden's writing partner on *A Game Plan for Life*. He told me, "Coach John Wooden's great-granddaughter teaches kindergarten in the Los Angeles public school system. She has one modest tattoo on her left arm, next to her wristwatch so she will see it often throughout the day. Coach, of course, is from a generation that regarded body art as the sort of thing you see on a sailor, not a kindergarten teacher or your great-granddaughter. So he was upset when someone told him about the tattoo.

"But Coach was very honored when he learned what the tattoo said: 'Make Each Day Your Masterpiece.' After all these years, the wisdom of Joshua Wooden is still being etched into the minds of his descendents—and even into their skin. That's powerful advice. If you've made each day your masterpiece, then by week's end, you've had a heck of a week."

In his book *Answers to Satisfy the Soul*, my writing partner Jim Denney observes that each and every day we all receive a free gift—ours to do with as we please. With each new morning, we receive the gift of 86,400 seconds, 86,400 ticks of the clock. We choose how to spend each second. We can invest each second, make it count, treat it as something rare and irreplaceable, or we can simply kill time.

"People say time is money," Denney writes. "I say time is life. . . . Ever hear someone say, 'I'm just killing time'? What is he really saying? 'I'm just killing myself.' Because time is all you have, and when it's gone, you're dead. When you kill time, you kill yourself, moment by moment, second by second, a little bit at a time."[1]

Coach Wooden understands the preciousness of a single second. In the game of basketball, time is everything. You've got four twelve-minute quarters to get the job done, forty-eight minutes to shoot more baskets than the other guy. As soon as the ball is inbounded, the shot clock starts ticking. You've got twenty-four seconds to shoot, or the ball turns over. The entire time you're dribbling, passing, and moving the ball, you face a determined opponent who blocks you, bumps you, puts his hand in your face, and tries to steal the ball—and the clock keeps ticking down. It's not easy to score under those conditions, but there's no finer feeling in the world than beating the buzzer and making that clutch shot. It's all in how you use your time.

Life is precious. Time is irreplaceable. You don't have a moment to lose. So make each day your masterpiece.

Devote a Portion of Each Day to Preparation

The late, great Alabama football coach Paul "Bear" Bryant understood what it means to make each day your masterpiece. In his office, he kept a framed plaque that served as a constant reminder to use each day's gift of 86,400 seconds to maximum effect. The plaque read: "What have you traded for what God has given you today?"

Greg Maddux is the only pitcher in Major League Baseball history to win at least fifteen games for seventeen consecutive seasons. He recalls some advice he once received from then-Cubs manager Tom Trebelhorn. "You know what the problem is with players these days?" Trebelhorn said. "They are always looking forward to something. They're never trying to do something today. They're always looking forward to the next off-day, the All-Star break, the end of the season. They never stop and enjoy the day that's here."

Maddux says that he thought about that and saw that Trebelhorn had a point. In fact, Maddux realized that he had that same mind-set of looking only to the future and never enjoying the present moment. From that day forward, Maddux concluded, "I started enjoying each day . . . and really started loving the games from that day on."[2]

Coach Wooden once explained what it means to make each day your masterpiece. "When I was teaching basketball, I urged my players to try their hardest to improve on that very day, to make that practice a masterpiece. . . . It begins by trying to make each day count and knowing you can never make up for a lost day." Whenever a player seemed to be dogging it in practice, Coach would tell him, "Don't think you can make up for it by working twice as hard tomorrow. If you have it within your power to work twice as hard, why aren't you doing it now?"[3]

Pete Blackman played basketball for Coach Wooden's Bruins from 1958 to 1962. He says that one key to Coach Wooden's success was that he made the most of each day through intense preparation. "Literally every practice was planned down to the minute," he told me. "You don't lose track of lessons like that. When you are preparing for a major business presentation fifteen years later, you look around, and you're probably the best prepared person there. Well, why is that true? Because people like Coach Wooden proved to you, at an early stage of development, that the time spent in preparation will pay off."

> *If you don't have time to do it right, when will you have time to do it over?*

Bill Walton has similar memories of Coach Wooden's practice sessions. He described those practices as "nonstop, electric, supercharged, intense, demanding." Coach Wooden would pace the sidelines, shouting encouraging slogans such as "Be quick—but don't hurry." Coach wanted his players to keep up a fast pace in practice so that on game day the tempo of the game would seem to be in a slower gear. Walton recalled that he and his teammates performed so well on game day because "everything we did in the games had actually happened faster at practice."

I once asked Coach Wooden what he meant by "Be quick—but don't hurry." He said, "You are more prone to making mistakes when you rush things. You must never allow yourself to be panicked or stampeded into going faster than your own tempo, but your tempo must be quick, or you won't get things done. I always found that quickness comes from preparation. When you have practiced and prepared yourself well, quickness comes naturally."

Coach Wooden learned the importance of preparation early in his coaching career. As a young basketball coach at South Bend High School, he became acquainted with Frank Leahy, the great Notre Dame football coach. Leahy invited Coach Wooden to visit a Notre Dame football practice, and from that practice Coach Wooden gained an unexpected wealth of ideas and insights about basketball. He saw how the Notre Dame players quickly transitioned from drill to drill as Leahy blew the whistle. The players responded automatically, like a well-oiled machine. Above all, Coach noticed that the Notre Dame players were quick, but they were never hurried. He made up his mind to apply those insights to his basketball practices, and that became Coach Wooden's system throughout his career.

In the early 1960s, Coach perfected an innovation in college basketball called the full-court press, a defensive strategy of pressuring the offense along the entire length of the court, both before and after the inbound pass. His teams picked up the tempo and became the quickest in the game, forcing their opponents to play at a faster tempo than they were used to. The quickness of Coach Wooden's teams forced their opponents to hurry—and make mistakes. Coach Wooden's quick-but-unhurried approach enabled him to win his first NCAA championship in 1964.

And the key to it all was preparation.

Swen Nater told me the story of Ralph Drollinger, the seven-foot-one-inch UCLA center whose presence made the crucial difference in the 1975 Final Four championship game against the University of Kentucky. Before Ralph could become a game-changer, Coach had to invest time in preparing Ralph Drollinger to play within the UCLA system—and preparing himself to coach Ralph Drollinger.

"As a high school player," Swen told me, "Ralph had developed a bad habit regarding defensive rebounds. If the opposing team shot and missed, and Ralph got the rebound, he'd hold the ball, then casually hand it off to a guard. Ralph had never learned the fast break in high school. He was used to a down-tempo game in which the guard walked the ball up the court.

"But walking the ball was not Bruins basketball. Coach was trying to teach Ralph the fast break—grabbing the defensive rebound then immediately passing the ball to the guard, who would race down the court at full speed. Ralph could not break his old slow-tempo high school habits, and it was driving Coach crazy. Coach never swore, of course, but I'm sure Ralph heard a frustrated Coach Wooden at the sidelines shouting, 'Goodness gracious sakes alive, Ralph! Pass the ball!' Ralph just couldn't learn Coach's approach.

"Coach Wooden was convinced that there *had* to be a way to get fast-break basketball across to Ralph Drollinger. He decided that the problem was not that Ralph couldn't learn but that he himself had not found the right way to teach the concept. So Coach decided to *prepare himself* and be ready for the next teachable moment.

> *Failure to prepare is preparing to fail.*

"One day at practice, Coach watched and waited for Drollinger to go up for the rebound, and at the exact moment Drollinger touched the ball, Coach shouted, 'Ralph! Pass it to somebody short!' Reacting by instinct to Coach's voice, Ralph did exactly as Coach instructed: He fired a quick pass to a guard. Coach waited for Drollinger's next rebound, and he shouted the same instructions to him again. And again.

"After just a few repetitions, Ralph had it down. He'd rebound, fire the pass, then sprint to the other basket without having to stop and think. Coach had found the key to teaching Drollinger the fast break.

"Wise teachers think ahead and prepare for teachable moments. I call this kind of preparation 'ready, set, teach.' If you want your players prepared to play, then you as the coach must be prepared to teach. Coach's ability to prepare himself so that he could prepare his players is one of the secrets to his phenomenal success as a teacher and coach. When you are prepared to make the most of every moment, you are ready to make the most of every day."

Louis Pasteur (1822–95), the French microbiologist, once said, "Fortune favors the prepared mind." In order to make each day your masterpiece, don't just flail away at the day's task. Invest some time and thought in preparation. A well-planned, well-prepared day can't help but be a masterpiece.

Set Goals to Make Each Day Your Masterpiece

Former UCLA player Jamaal Wilkes told me that, of the seven points of Joshua Wooden's creed, this principle—make each day your masterpiece—is his favorite. "All you can control is today," he said. "Yesterday is gone, and the future has not arrived yet. When you make the most of today, tomorrow will automatically be better. Coach lived this philosophy in front of us daily when we played for him at UCLA."

I interviewed Frank Arnold by telephone. When I called him, he said, "Pat, if I hadn't been here when you called, you would have gotten my voice mail. And you would have heard me say, 'Make it a great day.' Not, 'Have a great day,' but, 'Make it a great day.' That principle from the seven-point creed—make each day your masterpiece—tells me that the quality of my day depends on me. It's something I initiate. 'Have a great day' is a passive statement. But 'Make it a great day' means that I am in charge of making my day great. I learned that from Coach. Once we understand that truth, it changes the way we live our lives."

Ralph Drollinger told me, "John Wooden loved the word *industriousness*. It's important for me to go to bed at night knowing that I have worked as hard as I could, that I have done my very best that day. We leave our mark on the world every day, and in the process, we find satisfaction in our pursuits." Here are some ways we can take control of today—and turn this day into a masterpiece.

1. *Set clear goals, then take measurable steps toward achieving those goals.* Prioritize your goals for the day by writing a

things-to-do list. Tackle your first priorities first, then continue down the list.

If a task on your list seems too big and intimidating, break it down into a series of smaller, nonthreatening steps. For example, if your goal is to build a house, you might not even know where to begin. But if you break that goal into smaller, doable steps, your things-to-do list might say: Draw up plans. Obtain financing. Obtain a building permit. Purchase materials. Hire an electrician, plumber, roofer, painter, and other subcontractors. And so on and so forth.

Organize your tasks by laying them out on a timetable, setting reasonable deadlines. As you start carrying out the tasks on your things-to-do list, do one thing at a time, keep working at it until completion, cross it off your list, then move on to the next item.

2. *Put an end to procrastination.* People often say, "I'm going to do that someday, when I have more time." That day rarely comes. Most of us will never have more time than we have right now, so we need to stop wishing for "someday," stop making excuses and putting things off. Whatever you really want to accomplish, *do it now.*

Phil Brewer is a counselor in California. He once described a trip he took to Europe in the 1970s. "I went to Switzerland and interviewed several writers and thinkers, including Paul Tournier, the great Swiss psychiatrist," he recalled. "He said to me in his wonderful French-accented English, 'People are always looking for the right time and the perfect place to write, to paint, to accomplish some goal. They say, "I have to be in the mountains, I have to be on the coast, everything must be just so." But if you look at all the great achievements of history, you will see that they have largely been done in cold, cramped, unpicturesque conditions. Look where all the great people and all the great achievements have come from, and you see that they always seem to come from deprived situations.'

"It took me years to fully absorb the great truth that Dr. Tournier had given to me. I'm still absorbing it. I think he saw in me a perfectionist streak that so often keeps me from starting a project until just the right moment. I want a cup of coffee, but I want to drink it on the beach in Maui. The point is this: If you're going to write the great American novel, then write it. Don't put it off until everything's just so. Do it now."

3. *Beware of distractions and time wasters.* There are two kinds of distractions and time wasters. First, there are those we inflict on ourselves, such as internet surfing, unnecessary emailing or texting, unnecessary phoning, business meetings that have no point and accomplish little, watching mindless TV shows, playing video or computer games, or endlessly announcing every stray thought to the world via Facebook or Twitter. A cluttered living space or work space can also waste time, because clutter hinders the efficient use of time.

Second, there are the distractions and time wasters we allow others to inflict on us. Phone callers who will not hang up. Visitors who stay and stay and will not leave. People who ask us to volunteer our time when we really can't afford the time. (And because we are too weak-willed to say no, we say yes—then gripe and grumble about all the time we are wasting!)

All of these distractions and time wasters are intrusions we can control, at least to some degree. You can tell callers and visitors you need to get back to work. You can cut off your Facebook account. You can silence the phone and screen calls in order to meet your deadlines. You have more control over your schedule than you think you do. You just have to be willing to tell people, "It's been good talking to you, but I have to get back to work now." Then hang up the phone or chase them out of your office, and get back to work.

It's okay to say no when people intrude on your time, and you don't owe anyone an apology or an excuse. "I simply don't wish to do that" is a perfectly legitimate reason for saying no.

Don't make up a lie. Don't try to justify your decision. You have a right to determine how you will use your time. It's okay for you to invest your time pursuing your own goals instead of someone else's. You don't owe anyone an explanation.

4. *Make a time log.* This exercise is especially helpful when you know you are losing time, but you don't know where it is going. Divide a sheet of paper into thirty-minute blocks of time, from the time you get up until the time you go to sleep. At every thirty-minute block, jot a quick note (very brief, no more than five or six words) to indicate how you spent that half hour. Do this for a week, then take a good, hard look at how you are spending your time. This exercise will make you aware of how you organize, use, and waste time during the day. It will probably show you how, by making a few changes in your life, you can become more productive and effective in the use of your time.

5. *Focus on excellence.* If you want your day to be a masterpiece, use the hours in your day to produce works of excellence. Invest your time to create excellent work, to do excellent deeds of service for others, to make phone calls and write emails of excellence, to build excellent relationships with your spouse and children and friends. Never settle for second best. "Good enough" is never good enough. Only genuine excellence will do.

People have nicknamed Sue Enquist "the John Wooden of women's softball." She played softball for the UCLA Bruins from 1975 to 1978 (completing her college career with a .401 batting average) and returned to UCLA as an assistant coach in 1980. She was head coach of Bruins softball from 1989 to 2006, winning four NCAA championships as head coach. As both a player and a coach, Sue Enquist helped the Bruins win eleven NCAA softball titles, and she retired with an 887–175–1 career coaching record (.835 winning percentage). Sue Enquist established a record of excellence throughout her career.

Like Coach Wooden, Enquist focused less on winning *games* and more on a winning *attitude*. She would praise her players if they battled hard and lost, and she critiqued them mercilessly if they won with a lackluster effort. Like Coach Wooden, Enquist became famous for her sayings, which came to be known as "Sueisms." For example, "There are only two things you can control—your effort and your attitude." "I don't coach to the scoreboard, and they don't play to the scoreboard." And, "Leap into the unknown. If you fall, the team will pick you up."

Enquist's most famous Sueism is the 33 Percent Rule. According to this rule, you can divide the human race into three categories. The bottom third of people are whiners and complainers who suck the life out of you. The middle third are people whose attitude fluctuates from positive to negative depending on circumstances. The top third maintain a positive attitude even in adversity. These positive people in the top third are the leaders, the achievers, the game-changers.

The people in the top third strive for excellence at all times. They live in a "bubble" of high standards, Enguist says. Athletes who play on a team with other high-achieving, hardworking, positive-thinking teammates often do not realize what a rare experience that is. It is, she says, an "inside the bubble" experience. "The day you graduate and go out and get that job," Enquist adds, "watch how you're surrounded by the mediocre. You will be the standard others will emulate, which is an awesome compliment. You're going to learn how special it was to be in the bubble."

You, too, can live inside the bubble of excellence and high standards. You, too, can focus on excellence throughout your day. And if you focus on excellence from the moment you get up in the morning until you lie down at night, you will find that every day of your life is an experience of excellence—a day that is truly a masterpiece.

Each Day, Invest Yourself in Others

Swen Nater told me, "Playing for Coach was a boot camp for effective living. When he was coaching basketball, he was really teaching life. 'Make every minute count,' he'd say. 'Be productive. Build balance in your life. Keep your priorities in order.' But his most important teaching had to do with the Golden Rule and the way we are to treat other people.

"John Wooden's philosophy was that you have never lived a perfect day until you have helped someone who can never repay you in any way. John Wooden's goal was to live a perfect day—not once, but every single day. He really concentrated on that goal. I think that's why he was so open to meeting people at his condo, no matter who they were.

"Coach invested so much of his life in helping me. How can I ever pay him back? I can't! I can't even *begin* to pay him back. And that's how Coach wants it. That's how he chooses to live his life. He is always helping others, investing his life in others—and that's how he has made every day of his life a masterpiece."

One of John Wooden's most devoted disciples is UCLA gymnastics coach Valorie Kondos Field, known to her students as Miss Val. She was only fifteen when Coach retired from the sidelines in 1975, yet she has studied Coach's teaching methods, coaching philosophy, and leadership wisdom throughout her career. She has a profound respect for the seven-point creed Coach learned from his father. Perhaps that helps explain why her gymnastic teams have won five NCAA titles.

Not only is Miss Val a fan of Coach Wooden's, but Coach is a fan of Miss Val's. Until advancing years and declining health curtailed his activities, Coach had a regular spot at Pauley Pavilion for all the home meets of Miss Val and her gymnastics team—second row, floor level. John Wooden and Valorie Kondos Field share a common commitment to coaching as a form of teaching. Both coaches teach more than a sport. They teach *life*. As Miss Val explained:

> Gymnastics is an amazing venue through which to learn life lessons such as discipline, focus, and commitment to a goal. . . . One thing that we talk about a lot with our team . . . is the discussion of "learning" [and] "acquiring knowledge." . . . Going to class and studying isn't about making the grade but enriching your knowledge to help make living your life more colorful. It's about having an enthusiasm for learning about all sorts of different things in life. These always turn into interesting discussions with our team. . . . Regardless of what event they are on, or whether they are focusing on dance or gymnastics skills, the quality of their movement is what makes their movements come to life. This holds true in moving through daily life as well.[4]

John Wooden left a coaching and teaching legacy at UCLA that Miss Val carries on in the field of gymnastics. It's a legacy of instructing young athletes not only in the skills of competition but also in the life skills we all need to make each day a masterpiece.

I asked former UCLA player Brad Holland for his thoughts on this principle. "To me," he said, "making each day a masterpiece means living each day with joy and enthusiasm. When you live your life that way, you live each day to the fullest. That's how I want to live my life—focused on joy, focused on helping others, knowing I've spent my time on the things that matter most. Coach teaches us that it's not a perfect day unless you've done something for someone who cannot repay you. That's a great way to live your life."

One professional hockey player who lives this principle is Brooks Laich (pronounced "like"), the Canadian-born center of the Washington Capitals. The Capitals went into the 2010 play-offs with the best record in the NHL and a third straight division title. In the first four games of the quarterfinals against the Montreal Canadiens, the Capitals took a commanding 3–1 lead, but then the eighth-seeded Canadiens came back and won the next three games. On April 28, 2010, the Capitals lost the last game of the quarterfinals on their home ice with a score of 2–1. It was a heartbreaking way to end the season.

That night, Laich left the arena feeling that he and his teammates had let the fans down. Heading home, he crossed a bridge over the Potomac from D.C. into Virginia. Then he spotted a woman and her fourteen-year-old daughter beside the road with their disabled vehicle. He'd just suffered one of the worst disappointments of his career. He could have easily driven by.

But that wasn't his way. Laich pulled to the side of the road and got out. That's when he discovered that both mom and daughter were Capitals fans. They'd hit a pothole and blown a tire on their way home from the game.

The first thing Laich did was apologize to them for disappointing them with that loss. Then he got the jack and spare out of the trunk and spent the next forty minutes changing the tire. When he was finished, he sent them on their way.

Laich didn't do a good deed to get publicity. He didn't think anyone would ever hear about it. But the fourteen-year-old girl went straight home and posted the entire incident on her Facebook page. Within a few days, the story appeared in *USA Today*.

As Coach Wooden has said, "You have not lived a perfect day until you've done something for somebody who cannot repay you." Brooks Laich took one of the worst days of his life and turned it into a perfect day for a mother and her daughter. Though his team lost a shot at the championship, Laich made that day his masterpiece.[5]

He Wasn't Going to Leave Anything Unsaid

Ann Meyers Drysdale played women's basketball at UCLA. Talented and intensely competitive, she is the only woman ever to sign a player contract with an NBA team (the Indiana Pacers, 1979). She is the sister of former UCLA player Dave Meyers and the widow of L.A. Dodgers Hall of Fame pitcher Don Drysdale, who died in 1993. She was one of the best women basketball players ever to play the game, later enjoyed a successful career in television sports broadcasting, and now serves as the general manager of the Phoenix Mercury of the WNBA. Ann calls Coach Wooden "Papa."

She told me, "Papa has always shown a great admiration for his father. More than once, I've heard Papa talk about how hard his father worked and what a consummate gentleman he was. He says that he was always impressed that his father never had to raise his voice, yet he always commanded respect from the people around him.

"I grew up in a Catholic family where the Ten Commandments were the foundation of our home. The seven-point creed fits the Ten Commandments like a hand fits a glove. The principle that especially speaks to me is the principle of making each day your masterpiece. Every day is precious and irreplaceable to me. Over the years, I've lost a brother, a sister, and a husband. You never know what the next day will bring, so make today the best it can be. Papa teaches that the way to do that is to treat everyone with respect and try to love everybody, including the people who are hard to like. When I was a young athlete at UCLA, I saw how Coach lived out that creed every day without fail. The impact of his life has never left me."

Andy Hill recounted an incident that truly shows how each of us should make each day a masterpiece. "I was driving in my wife's car one day with Coach Wooden," Andy told me. "We were heading to a luncheon for an appearance. As I navigated the L.A. freeway system, out of the blue, Coach said to me, 'Andy, have I ever told you how much I love you?'

"I wasn't expecting that. I choked up and gripped the steering wheel tightly, not knowing what to say. Then Coach added,

'Have I ever told you how much I appreciate that you picked up the phone years ago and rebuilt our friendship?'

"At that, I almost drove off the freeway, but I didn't dare do any damage to my wife's new car. Thinking back, I realize that Coach doesn't do anything out of the blue. He had thought about what he wanted to say. He had made a decision that, on that day, he was going to tell me exactly how he felt about our friendship. He wasn't going to leave anything unsaid that ought to be said.

"I often think about that day, and Coach's words challenge me to give thought to the things I should do and say to make each day a masterpiece. That's what Coach Wooden's dad taught him so many years ago, and Coach is still passing that teaching along to others to this day."

After all these years, Joshua Hugh Wooden still challenges you and me today: Make each day your masterpiece by living wisely, living effectively, living joyfully, and living to invest each day of your life in the people around you.

5

Drink Deeply from Good Books, Especially the Bible

I have been in Coach Wooden's home several times. On each occasion, I have paused to admire the many books that line the walls of his home. Coach is a student of history, poetry, and great literature.

Former UCLA player Brett Vroman once told me that Coach Wooden's love of reading helped him recruit Vroman as a player. "I was one of the few players Coach Wooden ever came to personally recruit," he said. "We lived in Provo, Utah, and my mother was an English teacher. When Coach came into our home, he and Mom really hit it off, talking about English literature, reciting lines of poetry, and so forth."

Before Coach left their home, the Vromans said they couldn't imagine Brett playing for anyone but Coach John Wooden.

Another former UCLA player, Bill Johnson, told me, "One year at Christmas we took a road trip to Michigan State and

Bradley. A couple of us had to take an English Lit exam at the hotel, and Coach Wooden served as the proctor. I'll never forget how he talked with us about poetry and his love for the written and spoken word. He could have taught the course."

Coach's father, Joshua Hugh Wooden, could also have taught that course. After all, he was the one who first instilled a love for poetry and great literature in young Johnny Wooden. He was also the one who included this word of advice in his seven-point creed: Drink deeply from good books, especially the Bible.

In his own commentary on that creed, Coach observed, "Poetry, biographies, and all the other great books will greatly enrich your life. There are so many that are so good, and they will all be available to you. The poetry Dad read to us when we were kids instilled a love of reading. . . . Drink deeply from those great books of your own choosing and you will enrich yourself."[1]

The way Coach describes his family life in the early 1920s, you almost find yourself wishing you lived in an era before the invention of the internet, the Xbox, HD television, or iPhones. There were fewer distractions and there was a lot more time to spend with great literature. "We had no electricity, plumbing, or conveniences," Coach Wooden recalled, "and for entertainment Dad read books to us in the evening by the light of the coal-oil lamp. Sometimes we'd hear Lord Alfred Tennyson's *Idylls of the King*, Edgar Allan Poe's 'The Raven,' or even William Shakespeare. Before we were sent off to bed, he'd always include a verse or two from the Good Book."[2]

Joshua Hugh Wooden set a great example for his son Johnny, and John Wooden in turn set a great example for the young men he coached. Steve Jamison, longtime admirer and writing partner of Coach Wooden, told me, "I was never much of a reader as a young man, but Coach kept talking about how much he enjoyed reading Shakespeare and the Bible. He was a role model to me, someone I wanted to be like—and he was always talking about the books he read. When the man you most admire is both a reader and a real man, you think, *Well, why shouldn't I be a reader too? There must be something in all these books that is pretty important.* So that's how I became a reader. His example spoke to me in a powerful way."

Why Read?

Books are inexhaustible sources of knowledge and wisdom about life, the human condition, the world around us, history, philosophy, and more. In books, we find the lives of great leaders, successful entrepreneurs, brilliant thinkers, and people of action and accomplishment. Through the magic of books, we can experience thousands of lives, visit thousands of places, time travel through history, and explore an infinite array of ideas. Scottish literary historian Gilbert Highet said that books are not "lumps of lifeless paper, but minds alive on the shelves. From each of them goes out its own voice . . . and just as the touch of a button on our set will fill the room with music, so by taking down one of these volumes and opening it, one can call into range the voice of a man far distant in time and space, and hear him speaking to us, mind to mind, heart to heart."[3]

A library of good books is a wise collection of friends, mentors, counselors, advisers, and encouragers. Books instruct and entertain. Books affect the course of our lives. Charles W. Eliot, president of Harvard University in the late nineteenth and early twentieth centuries, put it this way: "Books are the quietest and most constant of friends; they are the most accessible and wisest of counselors, and the most patient of teachers."[4]

Many books have altered my own life in profound ways. The first such book was *Pop Warner's Book for Boys*, which

I read (and reread) when I was in elementary school. In that book, legendary football coach Pop Warner wrote, "If you're going to be a great athlete, you don't drink, you don't smoke, you get your rest." I bought into that message as a young boy and became fanatical about building good, healthy habits. That book is one of the reasons I've never taken up drinking or smoking.

I was also captivated by Bill Veeck's 1962 autobiography *Veeck as in Wreck*. I was fresh out of college and just beginning my pro sports career. Veeck's book challenged my thinking so dramatically that I made major life-altering decisions as I read. Later, I sought out baseball promoter Bill Veeck, and he invited me to his home for lunch. He became a friend and mentor to me. Every year, right to this day, I reread Bill Veeck's book as a reminder and a refresher.

Today, I read roughly three hundred books a year. I never go anywhere without a book, and if I go on long trips, I always pack half a dozen books in my suitcase. As I look around, I'm constantly amazed to find that many people actively *avoid* the pleasure of reading. I've noticed that when I go to a doctor's office or an airport lounge, the majority of people sit staring at the floor or texting on their phones or listening to their iPods—but hardly anyone reads. Why would people prefer to sit and space out instead of engaging heart, mind, and soul with a fascinating book?

> *The worst thing about new books is that they keep us from reading the old ones.*

The message Joshua Hugh Wooden gave his son Johnny in the 1920s is still true today: Don't just sip—*drink deeply* from great literature! Be thirsty for the knowledge and wisdom that can be found only in good books—and, of course, in the Good Book.

In many ways, Coach Wooden's father, Joshua Hugh Wooden, reminds me of Abraham Lincoln. Both were men of the soil, both were men of great physical prowess, both knew what it was like to be poor, and both had a deep love of books. I'm sure that Coach Wooden was aware of these Lincolnesque qualities in his father. Historian Gerald J. Prokopowicz wrote about the profound influence of books in Lincoln's life:

> There were few books in his house, but he studied these over and over, including the Bible, King James Version. As he gained access to books, such as *Pilgrim's Progress*, Aesop's *Fables*, *Robinson Crusoe*, and various histories, he devoured them as well. Neighbors remarked on his habit of reading while plowing and thought him lazy for it. He borrowed every book he could. He read Parson Weems's imaginative *Life of Washington*, with its invented episodes of the chopped cherry tree and the dollar thrown across the Potomac, and was so deeply impressed by Weems's description of the Revolution that he talked about it in 1861, on the eve of the Civil War: "I recollect thinking then, boy even though I was, that there must have been something more than common that those men struggled for." . . .
>
> Lincoln once borrowed a book from a neighbor and left it overnight in a crack between two logs in the wall of his cabin. An unexpected rain soaked the book through. Lincoln offered to pay for the damage by working for the neighbor, who rewarded him by giving him the book, one of the first he ever owned.[5]

The Roman educator Erasmus once said, "When I get a little money, I buy books. If any is left, I buy food and clothes." And Mark Twain observed, "The man who does not read good books has no advantage over the man who can't read them."[6]

My friend Brian Tracy, the noted self-help author, once told me that the highest-earning 10 percent of Americans read two to three hours a day. What do they read? Anything and everything that expands their knowledge and enables them to keep up with a fast-changing world: books, newspapers, and magazines. Brian says that, according to the American Booksellers Association, 80 percent of Americans have not read or purchased even one book during the past twelve months. The average American is simply not a reader. No wonder he's so average!

Anyone with a high school education can read a book a week. And what's a book a week? It's 52 books a year, or 520 books over the next decade. Just imagine how big your brain will be after you read 520 books! The benefits of reading are beyond numbering. Books increase your vocabulary, expand your knowledge, increase your critical thinking skills, and generally make you a wiser, more interesting, more thoughtful person.

Brian Tracy told me that if you read five books on any one subject, you can consider yourself a world-leading authority on that subject. So if you take his advice, you could become an authority on hundreds of subjects in a single decade. With all of that wisdom and knowledge crammed between your ears, you can't help being more effective and successful at anything you do.

Ten Tips for More Effective Reading

Dale Brown is the winningest coach in the history of men's basketball at Louisiana State University. He led the LSU Tigers to Final Four appearances in 1981 and 1986 and was twice named NCAA basketball Coach of the Year. Dale Brown and John Wooden are mutual admirers of each other. Coach Wooden once said, "If heads of states throughout this troubled world of ours had real concern and consideration for others as Dale Brown, I doubt if our racial, religious, and political problems would be a major issue."[7]

When I asked Dale Brown for his reflections on Coach Wooden, the first thing he mentioned was Coach's love of books. "John Wooden's condo is wall-to-wall books," he said. "Books are everywhere in his home, and they cover every topic. He has literally hundreds of books on Abraham Lincoln, one of his greatest heroes.

"One day I was with him along with a young high school coach. I made reference to something Coach had written in a book regarding high school coaches. I told Coach it was on page 75 of a certain book, and it had made a great impression on me. Coach Wooden said, 'No, Dale, it was on page 115.' Well, I was sure he was mistaken, but Coach said, 'Go to the other room, and look on the bottom shelf, the fifth book from the end, and check page 115.' I followed his instructions, and sure enough, there was the book, and there was the page, and there was the quote, spot on. I couldn't believe it—thousands of books in his home and he knew exactly where to find that quote."

Don Yeager was Coach Wooden's writing partner on *A Game Plan for Life*. Don told me, "I once looked around at the thousands of books in his library and asked him, 'How many of those books have you read?' He said, 'About 75 percent of them.' Now that he is age ninety-nine, his granddaughter reads to him. Even though he can't read them himself, he still loves books."

Coach Wooden was raised with a love of books, and he has always been able to get more out of books than any other human being I know. Let me share with you ten tips for reading books that will help you to become a more effective reader.

1. *Schedule a daily reading time, preferably an hour a day or more.* Don't have an hour, you say? Well, how much time do you spend watching TV or updating your Facebook page or playing Xbox or Wii? If you can't carve out an hour a day for reading, how about half an hour? Or a quarter hour? If you made a commitment to read even fifteen minutes a day—

and kept that commitment—it would add up to at least seven hours per month. That's a lot of reading, and those seven hours would make a big difference in your life.

2. *Be a discriminating reader.* When you *purchase* a book, you make a financial investment. When you *read* it, you invest something even more precious than money—your time and your life. So invest wisely. How do you find worthwhile books to read?

You can keep up with current releases through the *New York Times* book review or the review section of your local newspaper. Look up a favorite book on Amazon.com, and check out the titles under "Customers Who Bought This Item Also Bought . . ." For interviews and information on the latest books on history, culture, and politics, watch Book TV on the weekends on C-SPAN2.

Many people like to read books that are on the bestseller lists. Others prefer out-of-the-way niche books. I enjoy browsing in bookstores—walking the aisles and picking up the books and thumbing through them. I've found that, by scanning down the pages, I can always get a quick sense of whether it's the kind of book that speaks to me or not.

Ask for reading recommendations from people whose opinion you trust. Ask your minister, your professor, your doctor, your lawyer, or your children's teachers. When you see someone reading in the park or at the airport, stop and ask, "Is it good? What's it about? What do you like about it?" You'll usually find that "book people" love to talk about what they are reading.

Whenever you are introduced to someone new, here's a great conversation starter: "What books are you reading?" or "Who is your favorite author?" In fact, that's one of the fastest ways to truly get acquainted with someone. You can find out more about a person from the books they like to read than just about any other way. And in the process, you'll come away with recommendations for some books that just might change your life.

3. *Keep books handy wherever you are.* Never kill time. *Fill* your time with a good book. Keep a book with you wherever you go. Ever have trouble with insomnia? Keep a book by your bed. Do you ever have to spend time on hold, with your ear stuck to the phone? Read while you wait. Do you have a long commute twice a day? Listen to audio books in your car.

UCLA's Bill Bennett told me, "I learned from Coach Wooden that life is about continuous learning. If you're not learning, you are not living. So if you're wasting learning opportunities, you're wasting your life. Reading is one of the most learning-intensive activities you'll ever do. It doesn't matter if you are reading poetry or a great novel or a Shakespeare play or a book of history or biography— it's going to be a learning experience. It's going to enrich you and make you wiser. Coach would say, 'You never know it all.'"

It is what you learn after you know it all that counts.

4. *Don't just read books; interact with them.* Argue with them. Wrestle with them. Mark them up. Write your insights, questions, objections, and ideas in the margins. Use a pen or highlighter to mark passages that spark your thinking or challenge your cherished beliefs. As Roycroft Press founder Elbert Hubbard said, "I do not read a book. I hold a conversation with the author."

5. *Furnish your home with good books.* Yale professor William Lyon Phelps gave a radio talk on April 6, 1933, in which he spoke of the joys of his six-thousand-volume personal library:

> We enjoy reading books that belong to us much more than if they are borrowed. A borrowed book is like a guest in the

house. . . . You must see that it sustains no damage; it must not suffer while under your roof. You cannot leave it carelessly, you cannot mark it, you cannot turn down the pages, you cannot use it familiarly. And then, some day, although this is seldom done, you really ought to return it.

But your own books belong to you; you treat them with that affectionate intimacy that annihilates formality. Books are for use, not for show; you should own no book that you are afraid to mark up, or afraid to place on the table, wide open and face down. . . .

Everyone should begin collecting a private library in youth. . . . One should have one's own bookshelves, which should not have doors, glass windows, or keys; they should be free and accessible to the hand as well as to the eye. . . . Most of my indoor life is spent in a room containing six thousand books; and I have a stock answer to the invariable question that comes from strangers. "Have you read all of these books?" "Some of them twice." This reply is both true and unexpected.[8]

Fine books are worth keeping and rereading again and again throughout our lives. As novelist and playwright Robertson Davies once observed, "A truly great book should be read in youth, again in maturity, and once more in old age, as a fine building should be seen by morning light, at noon, and by midnight."[9]

6. *Set aside a portion of your vacation time for a reading sabbatical.* Instead of spending every day of your vacation traveling, hiking, sightseeing, spelunking, antiquing, or roller-coastering, save a few days for reading and reflection. This will give you time to decompress before returning to work. Instead of dragging into the office exhausted from your vacation, you'll arrive revived and refreshed, filled with new perspectives on life. Select some great fiction or nonfiction books that will give your soul a lift before you return to the real world.

Someone once said, "Trees give us two crucial elements for survival: oxygen and books." It's true. I rely on books in much the same way I rely on the oxygen in the air I breathe. So should you. Take an occasional reading sabbatical, and I guarantee you will feel more alive.

7. *Share your reading experiences with other enthusiastic readers.* Join a book discussion club, so you can read and discuss great literature with other book lovers. Or join an online book discussion group. Exploring books with other people will help you get more enjoyment and understanding out of the books you read. Antiquarian bookseller Nathan Pine once said, "There's something special about people who are interested in the printed word. They are a species all their own—learned, kind, knowledgeable, and human."[10]

8. *Use what you learn.* Take the insights and wisdom you gain from reading and use them in your conversations and daily life. When you use what you learn, you lock it into your long-term memory. Former UCLA player Dave Meyers told me, "I'm amazed at John Wooden's mind. He can memorize quotes, poems, and stories, then use them in speeches at the drop of a hat. Many of his players were students of language, and Coach loved those guys. Jamaal Wilkes and Coach would discuss great literature. Coach and Swen Nater were kindred spirits regarding poetry. Coach was always reading, and the stories and events he read about always showed up in his speeches and his daily conversation."

Speaking of Swen Nater, the former UCLA center told me, "Some people read without any sense of purpose. Coach Wooden was very purposeful in the way he read. He always read books that he thought would improve his life in some way, that would make him a better person. For example, he read a lot of biographies of great people. And then he would take what he had learned, and he would teach it to others.

"Sometimes people say, 'I can never remember a joke.' Well, that's because they never tell it. If you tell a joke over and over again, you remember it. It's the same with reading. If you take the stories, events, and ideas that you read about in books, and you are constantly sharing those insights with others, you remember them. They stay fresh in your mind. You have to keep using what you've learned."

9. *Widen your reading horizons.* Microsoft cofounder Bill Gates put it this way: "Read books on topics that don't pertain strictly to your business or industry. It's the best way to maintain a broad perspective."[11] Subjects and authors outside of your chosen field can challenge your thinking and reveal new solutions to seemingly insoluble problems.

Take, for example, the predicament faced by Kuwait City in 1964. Kuwait City sits on an inlet of the Persian Gulf. After the discovery of oil in the region in the 1930s, the ancient village of Kuwait quickly grew to become a thriving metropolis. The city's expanding population needed safe drinking water, which was first imported by barge from Iraq. In the 1950s, Kuwait City built a desalination plant to turn Persian Gulf salt water into drinkable freshwater.[12]

In 1964, disaster struck. A freighter, the *Al Kuwait*, overturned and sank in the Kuwait City harbor. The ship went down with a cargo of six thousand sheep, and all the sheep drowned. Worst of all, the ship went down not far from the water intakes of the desalination plant. The ship had to be raised quickly, before the toxins from the decomposing sheep began seeping out, but the ship had to be raised intact. If the hull was ruptured, the toxins would be released and sucked into the desalination facility, polluting the water supply.

Kuwait City put out a call for help. Danish engineer and inventor Karl Krøyer flew to Kuwait City with a plan to raise the ship. His plan was to pump millions of small balls made of polystyrene foam into the sunken ship. Polystyrene foam (better known by its trade name Styrofoam) is filled with tiny pockets of air. The buoyant polystyrene foam would displace the water, and the ship would gently rise to the surface.

Kuwaiti officials approved the plan, and Krøyer brought in equipment that formed the polystyrene balls at the site and continuously pumped them down a flexible hose into the hull of the wrecked freighter. Krøyer and his crew filled the uppermost deck first, then continued filling the lower holds until the ship rose gently to the surface and was towed away.

Where did Krøyer get his idea? Not from any textbooks on engineering. The idea came from a Danish edition of *Walt Disney's Comics and Stories*, which Krøyer reportedly read to his children. In one issue, Donald Duck and his three nephews had funneled Ping-Pong balls into a sunken yacht, forcing the boat to the surface. Krøyer proved that Donald Duck had the right idea. In fact, Krøyer later used the same technique to raise a Danish ship that had sunk in Sukkertoppen harbor in Greenland.[13]

The moral of the story: Don't confine your reading to a narrow range of interests. Brilliant ideas are everywhere, even in comic books. Read broadly, keep an open mind, and maintain a wide perspective.

10. *Encourage reading in others, especially the young.* As a parent, read to your children. As a teacher, encourage your students to discover the joy of reading. Make sure you continually present reading as a delight, not a chore. If you know a young person who doesn't like to read, find out what he or she enjoys most, then introduce that young person to a book that connects with his or her passion in life.

Andy Hill told me, "Coach appreciates literature, and we could all see how much he loves to read. When we were at UCLA, he didn't shove it at us. But we were enriched as young athletes by all the wisdom that Coach poured into us through his love of books."

The Wisdom of the Ages

In my book *Read for Your Life*, I tell the story of a woman whose life was literally saved by a book. University of Virginia women's basketball coach Debbie Ryan had celebrated her five hundredth career victory when, in August 2000, she was diagnosed with pancreatic cancer.

Upon hearing the diagnosis, she said that her first thought was, "'Well, I've had a good life. I'll see you all.' I knew that pancreatic cancer is pancreatic cancer." Doctors removed the tumor, and Ryan underwent six weeks of radiation and chemotherapy.

On the day she came home from the hospital, her cousin presented her with a copy of Lance Armstrong's *It's Not about the Bike*, in which Armstrong writes candidly about his biking career and his triumphant battle over cancer. "I read it cover to cover the first day. Stayed up all night," she said. "Reading his situation and knowing how grave mine was, it gave me so much motivation and hope. It's indescribable."

She followed doctors' orders to let her assistants handle recruiting chores, but she promised herself she would not let cancer keep her from coaching at practices and games. The following year, Debbie Ryan coached the U.S.A. women's basketball team to a gold medal at the Beijing World University Games.

Now more than ten years cancer free, Ryan says that Lance Armstrong's book enabled her to see her cancer from the perspective of a survivor instead of a victim. "When you're a cancer survivor," she said, "it's about knowing there are other people out there who have done it so you can feel like you can do it." She adds, "I've learned to reach out to other people in this same position, and to families who have loved ones in this position."[14]

Have you ever known anyone whose middle name was "Tremendous"? Charlie "Tremendous" Jones was the most positive, inspiring person I've ever encountered. I first met him in Philadelphia in 1968. Over the years, I saw him often and spoke at events he put on. We remained friends for forty years. He always called me, "Tremendous Pat!" Charlie was a big guy, about six feet, five inches, and his trademark was his hug. Whenever you saw him, you knew that a big bear hug was coming—and you'd better keep your arms at your sides to protect your ribs!

Charlie was a highly successful real estate salesman who retired at age thirty-seven and became one of the top motivational speakers in the world. Wherever he went, he fired people up with optimism, enthusiasm, and a love of books. His own book, titled *Life Is Tremendous*, sold more than two million copies. Back when he was just plain Charlie Jones, he would sign his letters "Tremendous, Charlie Jones," so people started calling him Charlie "Tremendous" Jones, and the name stuck. He once wrote, "You are the same today as you're going to be in five years except for two things, the people you meet and the books you read."[15]

When his son Jerry was sixteen, Charlie made him an offer. He would help Jerry earn money to buy a car. All Jerry had to do was read certain books and write a book report. Charlie would pick the books—motivational books, history books, biographies, and inspirational books—and whenever Jerry turned in a book report, Charlie would deposit money in his car fund. The books Charlie selected for his son ranged from Dale Carnegie's *How to Win Friends and Influence People* to the Old Testament book of Joshua. "In two years," Charlie told Jerry, "if you read in style, you'll drive in style. But if you read like a bum, you're going to drive like a bum."

The result: Charlie's teenage son developed an insatiable hunger for reading. The boy could not stop talking about the latest books he had read. After reading enough books to buy a car, Jerry surprised his dad: "He kept the money and used my car and my gas." The young man graduated from high school and went off to college. Every so often he wrote his father a postcard, describing the latest books he had read and insights he had gained. Charlie's son would sign his postcards, "Tremendously, too. Jerry."

Charlie recalled his reaction when he read those cards. "I would put my head on my desk and cry. Do you know why? He was thinking thoughts that I never dreamed a young person could think."

When Charlie "Tremendous" Jones became a grandfather, he began influencing his grandchildren in the same way. On one Father's Day, he wrote a letter to his nine-year-old grandson Sammy, and his message to Sammy is one that you and I should take to heart:

> Read, read, read, read. A proper diet is good for your body, and the best books are good for your mind. . . . Read biographies, autobiographies and history. Books will provide many of the friends, mentors, role models and heroes you will need in life. Biographies will help you see that there is nothing that can happen to you that wasn't experienced by many who used their failures and tragedies and disappointments as stepping stones for more tremendous lives. Many of my best friends are people I've never met—Oswald Chambers, George Mueller, Charles Spurgeon, A.W. Tozer, Abraham Lincoln, Jean Gietzen, hundreds of others. . . . God's greatest gift for our time on earth is His Word.[16]

Charlie said a tremendous mouthful! If the wisdom of the ages is found in books, then the greatest wisdom of all is found in the Bible. Charlie, Coach Wooden, and Pat Williams are all convinced that the Bible is the inspired Word of God. That book has completely transformed my life as I have read it, studied it, and memorized passages from it. Those who know Coach Wooden testify to the profound influence of that book on his life.

The Companionship of Good Books

Frank Arnold was an assistant to Coach Wooden from 1971 to 1975. He told me, "When I was with Coach, he read the Bible every day. He did this his whole life. He kept his worn and well-used Bible on the desk in his office, and sometimes when his players came by and had to wait for him, they'd pick up the Bible and read from it. It always pleased Coach to see his players reading from his Bible."

Coach's former assistant Jay Carty told me, "When I was working under Coach Wooden, he would start and end each day with the Bible." Former player Dave Meyers said, "When you analyze the seven-point creed carefully, all of these principles come right out of the Bible." And Elmer Reynolds, longtime Martinsville resident and friend of the Wooden family, told me, "As I've studied John Wooden's many tributes to his father, I see that they are based on the Bible. That verse about honoring your father and mother so your days will be long on the earth says it all. Coach received the seven-point creed from his father when he was just a youngster. Now, at almost a hundred years of age, he still honors his father and lives by that creed."

Coach Wooden's love of books in general, and the Bible in particular, impacted the lives of those he taught. Brad Holland told me, "There is so much to be learned from the written word and from the Word of God. The Bible has stood the test of time to be the truth." And Ralph Drollinger said, "Reading is the key for me and does so much for my thinking process. I like to hide in good books, especially the Bible. God's Word is a preserving agent to fight off the corrosive influence of this world."

At the close of the apostle Paul's second letter to his young friend Timothy, he writes, "Do your best to come to me quickly, for Demas, because he loved this world, has deserted me and has gone to Thessalonica. Crescens has gone to Galatia, and Titus to Dalmatia. Only Luke is with me. Get Mark and bring him with you, because he is helpful to me in my ministry. I sent Tychicus to Ephesus. When you come, bring the cloak that I left with Carpus at Troas, and my scrolls, especially the parchments" (2 Tim. 4:9–13 NIV). At the end of his life, as he was in chains in prison in Rome, facing a cold winter and execution by beheading, the apostle Paul sought consolation in only two things: the companionship of his friends and the companionship of his books.

Books are our friends—and our best friend of all is the Bible. In its pages, we find not only insight and knowledge but also comfort for the soul. Throughout your life, in the good times and the hard times, heed the counsel of Joshua Hugh Wooden: Drink deeply from good books, especially the Bible.

6

Make Friendship a Fine Art

Bill Walton once shared with me a story that illustrates the paradox of his coach-player relationship with Coach Wooden. "At UCLA," Bill said, "I received a lot of awards, and the different organizations that gave me the awards would want me to go to a dinner, receive the award, and give a little speech. I hated that, and I told Coach I wasn't going. He said, 'Bill, you have to go.' I said, 'But Coach, I can't speak in front of people. I stutter and stammer. I'll embarrass myself. I'll embarrass you and UCLA.' He said, 'You still have to go.'

"I wasn't going to win this argument. So I made a deal with Coach. I said, 'Okay, I'll go, but you make the speech so I don't embarrass myself and everyone else.' Coach agreed.

"We headed out on our first trip. We boarded the flight and sat in first class, Coach on one side of the aisle and me on the other. The flight attendant came by to take our drink orders. 'What will you have, Coach Wooden?' He ordered black coffee. 'And you, Mr. Walton?' I said, 'I'll have a beer.'

"Coach leaned over to the flight attendant and said, 'No, he won't.' And that's how that trip began. Coach was my friend and mentor, but it was a friendship with a certain distance—the distance imposed by his authority over me as my coach.

"My relationship with Coach changed dramatically the moment I stopped playing for him. He then became a friend. But while we were players, it was all about our growth and development as players and as human beings. He was always pushing us to be the best we could be. We were terrified to talk with him at UCLA. He was like the school principal, the disciplinarian. He was not your friend, in the sense of a friend you can be at ease around. Today he's that kind of friend to me, but not back then. That kind of friendship would come later."

Some players, however, found it hard to make a complete transition from a player-coach relationship to a friend-friend relationship. One of those players was Eddie Ehlers, who played basketball for Coach Wooden at Indiana State in the late 1940s. Several years after Ehlers left State and began a career in professional sports, he came back to Terre Haute to visit Coach Wooden. The two men chatted for a few minutes, then Ehlers said, "Coach, do you mind if I call you John?"

"No, Eddie," Coach Wooden replied. "I think that would be fine."

Eddie seemed pleased. "Well, John, it's like this. Things have been going pretty well for me, John. . . ." And he continued on like that for about five minutes, calling his former coach "John" a dozen times or so.

Finally, Ehlers stopped and shook his head. "I can't do it," he said. "I've tried, but I just can't call you John. It's going to have to be Coach."[1]

In his biography of John Wooden, Neville Johnson said that Coach Wooden had an open-door policy with his players. They all had his home phone number, which they could use

118

at any time, but in reality, comparatively few players developed such a close friendship with Coach that they spent time visiting with him in his home. The coach-player relationship is a kind of friendship, yet the coach's authority imposes an element of distance on the relationship. One of Coach Wooden's former assistants, Frank Arnold, put it this way: "He was close to the players, but not that close. He had a closeness that was very meaningful. They weren't fearful of him; I think a better way to put it is that they were in awe of him."[2]

Some Tips on the Fine Art of Friendship

"When we were at UCLA," Bill Walton told me, "Coach Wooden never talked to us about himself or his life before coaching. There were no family references, no mentions of his father. During the UCLA glory years, it was all about preparing us to play and preparing us for life. John Wooden was the teacher and we were the pupils. Only after I left UCLA did I begin to learn about Coach's father and the seven-point creed. Only then did I begin to learn Coach's views on matters like friendship, and I began to see how those beliefs shaped the life of the man who had been my coach."

"Make friendship a fine art," Joshua Wooden once told his son Johnny. What did Coach's father mean? Why should anyone have to make a "fine art" of friendship? Doesn't friendship happen naturally? We all have friends. I do, you do, everybody does.

Or do we? Do we all have deep, lasting friendships? Or do we merely hang out with a bunch of shallow, superficial acquaintances?

When Joshua Wooden gave this advice to his son, he wasn't saying, "Make a lot of friends." He was saying, "Cultivate close, meaningful friendships. Work at being a great friend to others." How do we do that?

In *Wooden: A Lifetime of Observations and Reflections On and Off the Court*, Coach explains what it means to make friendship a fine art: "Don't take friendship for granted. Friendship is giving and sharing of yourself. . . . Someone is not a good friend because he or she does good things for you all the time. It's friendship when you do good things for each other. It's showing concern and consideration. . . . The first and most important step in friendship is being a friend."[3]

Coach tells us that the gold standard for friendship is the kind of relationship he and his wife, Nell, had for so many years. "Friendship," he once wrote, "is like a good marriage— it's based on common concern. Friends help each other; they don't use each other. . . . If we use our friends to advance a personal agenda, we'll never have inner peace. Friends help to complete us, and we'll be better for having taken them along on our journey."[4]

Former UCLA center Swen Nater told me, "Friendship is a matter of give-and-take. If you only give or only take, the relationship becomes unbalanced and out of bounds. The fine art of friendship is not a one-way street. Good friends know how to go through tough times together. They know how to give and how to receive."

Genuine, meaningful friendship is rare. To be a genuine friend, demonstrate a genuine interest in the things that interest your friends. Dale Carnegie once observed, "You make more friends by becoming interested in other people than by trying to interest other people in yourself."[5]

Good friends are good listeners. They cultivate the art of getting others to talk about themselves. They ask open-ended questions that lead to discussion. Mark Gottfried, former UCLA assistant and longtime basketball coach at the University of Alabama, told me, "Coach Wooden is a role model of genuine friendship. A big part of it is how well Coach listens to people. He asks probing questions and gets people to talk about what's really going on in their lives. He's a great listener. Coach has taught me so much about friendship."

A good friend makes others feel important. Coach Wooden always finds ways to let others know they matter to him. Let people know they are important to you, and you will build important friendships.

A great way to cement the bond of friendship is to call your friends by name. Don't overdo it, but do it. An embrace, a touch on the arm, and the sound of your friend's name are points of contact that establish a sense of connection and intimacy with your friend.

Devote quality time to building quality friendships. Ralph Drollinger told me, "It takes discipline and sacrifice to build a friendship—and that takes time. But it's so easy to blow out a friendship; it can be ruined so quickly. We must serve our friends and build equity with them over time. That truly is a fine art."

You don't have to agree with your friends. In fact, genuine friendship transcends differences of opinion. To be a good friend, respect your friend's right to hold a viewpoint different from your own. If you look back over the course of your deepest friendships, I think you'll find that those friendships were founded on similarities, but they have been held together by a respect for differences. As Mark Twain once said, "The proper office of a friend is to side with you when you are in the wrong. Nearly anybody will side with you when you are in the right."[6]

To be a genuine friend, care enough to confront your friends when they are going astray. Friends don't let friends harm themselves or others. When you feel you need to confront a friend, make sure you do so only out of genuine love and caring for that person. If you take any pleasure in criticizing your friends, you have the wrong attitude—and you'll damage your friendship. The Bible tells us, "As iron sharpens iron, so one man sharpens another" (Prov. 27:17 NIV). True friends care enough to sharpen each other.

The art of friendship requires us to be open-minded toward each other. So learn to see reality from your friend's point of view. You don't have to agree. Just try to understand. Albert Camus said, "Don't walk in front of me; I may not follow. Don't walk behind me; I may not lead. Just walk beside me and be my friend."[7]

To be a true friend, show that you care. Be there for your friends when they need you. Celebrate the joys and triumphs in the lives of your friends. Share your friends' struggles when they hurt. As Oprah Winfrey once said, "Lots of people want to ride with you in the limo, but what you want is someone who will take the bus with you when the limo breaks down."[8]

Brad Holland put it this way: "How many friends can you truly count on? I want to be that person to my friends. That's what it means to make friendship a fine art. I want to be the person who will give the shirt off my back to a friend in need. I want my friends to know that I will always be there for them."

Our pride sometimes gets in the way of friendship. It's often easier to be the friend who gives than to be the friend who receives. It is humbling to be on the receiving end of friendship, yet true friends do not hesitate to give or to receive. When you go through tough times, don't be too proud to let your friends help you. That's what friends are for.

When a friend is going through a time of loss or grief, it means a lot for you simply to be there at that time. You may think, *But I don't know what to say at a time like that.* The truth is, no one does. And that's okay. Don't feel you have to fill the silence with talk. Fill it with your quiet presence. That will be enough.

Henri Nouwen put it this way:

When we honestly ask ourselves which person in our lives means the most to us, we often find that it is those who, instead of giving advice, solutions, or cures, have chosen rather to share our pain and touch our wounds with a warm and tender hand. The friend who can be silent with us in a moment of despair or confusion, who can stay with us in an hour of grief and bereavement, who can tolerate not knowing, not curing, not healing, and face with us the reality of our powerlessness, that is a friend who cares.[9]

To be a good friend, always protect the reputation of your friends. Never break a confidence. Never gossip or embarrass your friends. When others gossip or criticize friends in your presence, stand up for them and defend them.

When a true friend makes a mistake or hurts your feelings, be quick to forgive and be ready to forget. As someone once said, "Real friends are those who, when you've made a fool of yourself, don't feel you've done a permanent job."

One of Coach Wooden's heroes is Abraham Lincoln. On one occasion, President Lincoln was at his desk in the White House, sorting through appeals for presidential pardons. Usually, when a convicted prisoner requests executive clemency, he includes letters from friends who will vouch for his character and plead for mercy. But President Lincoln was surprised to see one application for pardon without a single letter of support from friends.

"What?" asked Lincoln. "Has this man no friends?"

"No," said the president's aide, "he hasn't a single friend."

"Then I will be his friend," said the president, and with that, he signed the pardon.[10]

To be a true friend, be an encourager and a cheerleader. Tell your friends you believe in them. Urge them to persevere through trials and problems. Tell them you're cheering for them all the way to the finish line. Help them any way you can.

Above all, tell your friends how you feel about them. Don't save your eulogies for your friends' funerals. Whatever ought to be said, *say it now*. Tomorrow might be too late.

The Fine Art of Choosing Friends Wisely

Whether in college or in the pros, the life of an athlete is like a minefield, filled with moral and spiritual explosive devices. Peter Boulware, a former NFL linebacker who played his entire pro career for the Baltimore Ravens, was well aware of the dangers all around him. So Boulware relied on close friendships with other Christian athletes to protect himself against temptation. While playing football at Florida State, he found another player who shared his Christian values: defensive end Andre Wadsworth.

"Andre and I are both Christians," Boulware later observed. "Our faith is what we've built our lives on and what has given us the courage and strength to overcome limitations. It has also given us the basis for a solid, lasting friendship."

They studied the Bible together, prayed together, and held each other accountable for maintaining their moral integrity. They gave each other permission to ask the hard questions and demand truthful answers. "We have the same spiritual beliefs and the same values," Boulware said. "We had a good impact on each other in college. . . . There are a lot of people pulling at you to do the wrong things. And it's tough by yourself when you're trying to live right and do the right thing. But Andre and I would encourage each other and keep each other accountable. When we would see the other person do something that violated our standards, we would say, 'I don't think you should be doing that,' or 'I see that you're struggling here. How can I help?'"

At the end of their college careers, Boulware and Wadsworth were drafted by different NFL teams—Boulware by the Ravens, Wadsworth by the Arizona Cardinals. Boulware missed that daily connection with Wadsworth, but he made it a priority to choose new friends who would help him maintain his integrity and moral standards. "I still find it essential to have other Christians who encourage me and challenge me the same way Andre did when we were in college," he said. "I choose my closest friends by looking at the way they're living. I want to learn from people who are living out what they know is right and not just talking about it."[11]

> *What you are as a person is far more important than what you are as a basketball player.*

Andy Hill told me, "Coach Wooden was focused on character development. He talked about the importance of choosing your friends wisely and making sure you have friends who care enough to challenge you and ask you the tough questions: Are you working on becoming more patient and self-controlled? Are you overcoming bad habits? Are you being honest with yourself? Bad friends tear you down. Good friends build you up. People who are focused on continuous improvement want to have good friends in their lives, holding them accountable for their character growth."

And Jamaal Wilkes told me, "The fine art of friendship means that I should have the finest of friends who want me to be the best I can be, and I should be motivated to give something extra back to my friends."

Teach Your Children the Fine Art of Friendship

I once interviewed Steve Reed, a pastor and author of *The Suffering Clause: A Leader's Surprising Secret for Outlasting Tough Times.* He told me a story about teaching his son the importance of making good choices when making friends. "My middle son, Zach, was about ten or eleven," Steve said, "and he was letting his friends talk him into getting in trouble at school. One day, Zach's teacher called. When we confronted Zach, he said his friends were to blame. 'They talked me into it,' he said.

"I told him, 'Zach, from this point on, you're a leader, not a follower. Your friends aren't in charge of your behavior— you are. You need to be an influence on your friends, not the other way around. If you try to blame them for your actions, I won't buy it. You are now the leader of your friends.'

"He said, 'But Dad, I don't want to be the leader!'

"'You have no choice, Zach. When you're with your friends, you must lead by example.'

"That wasn't easy for Zach, but he worked at it and really made strides. In time, he invited his friends to our church youth group. Soon, two of Zach's friends had committed their lives to Jesus Christ."

Steve Reed taught his son Zach an important lesson in the fine art of friendship: Genuine friends lift each other up; they don't drag each other down. True friends bring out the best in each other.

High school English teacher Kathy Megyeri spent more than three years shaping young lives in the Washington, D.C., area. She told me about an assignment she had given to her students. "We had just finished reading Harper Lee's *To Kill a Mockingbird*," she said. "In that book, the protagonist, Atticus Finch, tells his daughter Scout, 'You never really know a man until you stand in his shoes and walk around in them.'"

Megyeri gave her students an assignment to write down a set of rules to define how they could become people of good character, people who would truly be good friends to others. When her students turned in their assignments, Megyeri was amazed at the mature wisdom they expressed. One student offered a list of rules in the form of a wall poster. Those rules included:

- Knowing many people is far better than knowing only yourself.
- Never lose a friendship because true friendships are rare.
- When someone asks, "Do I have food on my face?" don't lie. Tell them. You wouldn't want anything on your face.
- Let people help you.
- Spend time getting to know your parents.
- When saying "I love you," mean it; that's the most important phrase in your life.

That is one high schooler who is wise in the art of friendship. Whether you are a parent, teacher, coach, or mentor, encourage your kids and students to think seriously about the art of friendship and to define rules that will make them wise in the ways of choosing good friends and maintaining strong friendships.

The Fine Art of Resolving Conflict

What about conflict? How should good friends deal with disagreements?

This too is a fine art. There are disagreements in every friendship, and disagreements easily turn into arguments. "When we become argumentative," Coach Wooden says, "we tend to lose control." And disagreements that spin out of control turn into fights. Those who have mastered the fine art of friendship know how to disagree without being disagreeable.

John Wooden's best friend throughout his life was his wife, Nell. On most occasions, John and Nell were able to resolve

127

their differences without arguing or fighting. But at the beginning of World War II, they had a disagreement that seemed to have no solution. Soon after the attack on Pearl Harbor, John Wooden decided to enlist in the military and fight for his country. Nell didn't want him to go. Because Coach was a teacher and the father of two young children, he could get an exemption from the draft, yet he felt very strongly that it was his duty to serve. So he enlisted in the navy. "Nellie may not have fully understood my decision to enlist," Coach recalled, "but she came to accept it."

Coach recalls another time when he and Nell had a disagreement that turned disagreeable. It was one of the few times in Coach's life that he got so angry he actually had to leave the house to cool off. "When I got home," he recalled, "there was a card on my pillow. On the card Nellie had written: 'Don't try to understand me, just love me.' It was a lesson I needed to learn."[12]

In 1982, while undergoing hip replacement surgery, Nell suffered a heart attack. She remained in a coma for three months, then regained consciousness and returned home. She slowly improved, though she never fully recovered her former strength. Early on Christmas morning, 1984, she suffered another setback, which left her semicomatose for three months. She passed away on March 21, 1985. On that day, Coach recalls, "God relieved Nellie of her suffering and I lost my life partner."[13]

Ever since Nell passed away, Coach Wooden has observed the twenty-first day of every month by sitting down at his desk and writing a love letter to her. He tells her how much he loves her, misses her, and looks forward to seeing her again. He puts each letter in an envelope and places it on a stack of love letters that sits on the pillow on her side of the bed. Coach took me into that bedroom one time, and I got a lump in my throat when I saw that enormous yet neat bundle of love letters, tied with a yellow ribbon. Coach sleeps only on his side of the bed and leaves her side undisturbed. Next to Nell's pillow lies the packet of love letters, plus one other thing: the card that Nell wrote to him so many years ago after their argument, the card that reads, "Don't try to understand me, just love me."

Some would say that John Wooden was lucky to have married his best friend. But I don't think luck had anything to do with it. I'm convinced that John and Nell worked very hard at making their friendship work.

Their love outlasted life itself because John and Nell made friendship a fine art.

7

Build a Shelter against a Rainy Day by the Life You Live

In July 2000, I checked my voice mail and heard these soft-spoken words: "Mr. Williams, this is John Wooden, former basketball coach at UCLA." I was awestruck: The most legendary coach in sports history actually thought he needed to remind me of who he was!

In the rest of the message, he gave me his personal recommendation for a UCLA trainer who had applied for a position with the Magic. He concluded with these words: "I have enjoyed reading your books very much. Good-bye."

The humility of Coach Wooden is not false humility; it's absolutely genuine. Every time I'm in Coach's presence, I marvel at the gently self-effacing nature of his character and at his amazing ability to instill traits of humility and unselfishness in his players—qualities that are so underappreciated today yet had so much to do with all those winning streaks and championship seasons.

In our age, ego and arrogance are celebrated, and humility is often confused with self-abasement. But when a rare human being like Coach Wooden comes along, the entire world stops and takes notice. He always seemed genuinely embarrassed when people praised him for his accomplishments. For example, at one speaking appearance, the emcee gave Coach an introduction filled with praise and plaudits, and when Coach finally got up to speak, he said, "I hope the good Lord will forgive my introducer for over-praising me, and me for enjoying it so much."[1]

> *Much can be accomplished by teamwork when no one is concerned about who gets credit.*

It has been said that genuine humility doesn't make you think less of yourself; it simply makes you think of yourself less. You can be quite humble yet still have a healthy sense of self-esteem. In fact, the most humble people I've met generally have the most dynamic and impressive personalities. Arrogance and vanity are off-putting and unpleasant to be around. True humility is one of the most attractive qualities any human being can possess.

Reporter Jim O'Connell of the Associated Press once interviewed Coach, referring to him as a "legend" and calling him by a nickname the sports press had given him, "The Wizard of Westwood." Coach told O'Connell, "I'm no legend and I am embarrassed about that. I don't like the 'Wizard' [title] at all. I don't like false modesty. I'm proud of the fact that I was fortunate to have a lot of wonderful players who brought about national championships and that I'm a part of that. . . . But I'm also realistic, and I know that without those players it wouldn't have happened."[2]

Coach always deflected glory away from himself and onto his players. And while it is true that it is ultimately the players who go on the court and win (or lose) basketball games, the most talented team in the world can't win without great coaching. When Coach Wooden became head coach of the UCLA Bruins in 1948, he took charge of a struggling basketball program with a 12–13 losing record. In a single year, he turned the Bruins into 22–7 division champions—up to that time, the most wins in a single season since UCLA's basketball program began in 1919. So while Coach Wooden humbly gives his players the glory, he certainly deserves credit for UCLA's amazing turnaround and unparalleled success.

Proof of the genuineness of Coach's humility is the fact that his humble spirit is on display even when he doesn't know anyone is watching. College basketball coach Bob Burke told me, "Back in the 1960s, I was working on the staff at the Campbell University summer camp. On the first day, I went out early to get oriented, and there was John Wooden, championship coach, sweeping the floor all by himself."

As longtime Martinsville resident Elmer Reynolds told me, the pattern for John Wooden's humility was his father, Joshua Hugh Wooden. "Johnny Wooden learned humility by watching his father," Reynolds told me. "Johnny saw how his father responded when he lost the farm and had to spend the last fifteen years of his life in the steamy, unpleasant environment of the mineral baths of the sanitarium. John Wooden's dad had the humble heart of a servant—and so does Johnny. Joshua Wooden told his son to build a shelter against a rainy day by the way he lives his life, and one way John Wooden does that is by living a truly humble life—the life of a genuine servant."

When Joshua Hugh Wooden gave his son the sixth principle of his seven-point creed—build a shelter against a rainy day—he offered no explanation as to what kind of "shelter" he meant. At first glance, you might think that John Wooden's father was giving wise financial advice to his sons, and I truly believe that Joshua Wooden *did* want his sons to handle their finances wisely. The advice to build a shelter against a rainy day can definitely apply to the most practical dimension of our lives, and we will look at that dimension in just a moment.

But in his own commentary on the sixth principle, Coach John Wooden wrote, "This is not necessarily a material shelter."[3] Coach's father specifically said, "Build a shelter against a rainy day *by the life you lead.*" The way we build a shelter against a rainy day is not primarily by accumulating assets but by *becoming a certain kind of person.* So the issue here is not one of accumulating material possessions but one of accumulating values, virtues, character traits, faith in God, strong family relationships, and enduring friendships. These are the "possessions" that will help us survive the rain storms and floods of life.

A Shelter of Values and Character

John Wooden and his brothers grew up poor but without any sense of being deprived. Johnny's mother, Roxie Anna Wooden, made all of her children's clothes and never bought a new dress for herself. On those rare occasions when she bought new shoes, she made sure they lasted a long time. Joshua and Roxie Wooden raised most of their own food on the farm. Coach Wooden remembers that most of the vegetables his mother raised went straight from her garden to the family dinner table or were canned and stored in Mason jars in the cool, dark cellar.

Those rows of jars were like money in the bank for a rainy day. The vegetables John Wooden's mother canned in the summertime served as a powerful symbol in his life. When the rainy season came, his mother could go down into the cellar, select one of those Mason jars, and serve her family the bounty of summertime. So when John Wooden's father gave him that piece of paper with the advice, "Build a shelter against a rainy day by the life you live," John had a vivid mental image of what that means.

Your character and your values are like vegetables that grow in the sunshine, which you can store away in the cellar of your soul. They will always be there to feed on in the lean times, the rainy seasons of life. Strong values and strong character give you the ability to make wise decisions in rainy-day situations. As Walt Disney's brother and business partner, Roy O. Disney, once said, "It's not hard to make decisions when you know what your values are."[4]

Examples of some of the values and character traits that strengthen us against the rainy seasons of life include integrity, a strong work ethic, and persistence. Coach Wooden had these qualities in abundance. From the earliest days of his career, it was clear, first of all, that Coach John Wooden was a man of unyielding integrity.

In 1948, while teaching and coaching at Indiana State Teachers College, Coach received two offers for head coaching positions—one at the University of Minnesota, the other at UCLA. He really wanted to stay in the Midwest, so he was eager to accept the position at Minnesota. However, there were some personnel issues that needed to be worked out before he could accept the offer. The Minnesota board of directors had to meet and formally approve the changes Coach wanted.

At the same time, UCLA was pressing Coach for an answer. So Coach arranged to have the University of Minnesota call him at 6 p.m. on a Saturday night, and UCLA would call him at 7 p.m. This way, he would know whether he had a firm offer from Minnesota before UCLA called.

Saturday night came, and Coach patiently waited for the call from Minnesota, but 6 p.m. came and went, and the phone did not ring. Finally, at 7 p.m. on the dot, the phone rang. It was UCLA, calling at the appointed time, offering Coach the job in California. Concluding that Minnesota had decided not to offer him the job, Coach agreed to accept UCLA's offer.

No sooner had Coach hung up the phone when it rang again. It was the University of Minnesota. An ice storm across the state of Minnesota had knocked out the phone lines. The Minnesota board had been trying since 6 p.m. to get through to Coach Wooden. When phone service was finally restored, it was almost 7:30 p.m. The University of Minnesota had agreed to all of Coach Wooden's conditions, and the job was his if he said yes.

This was the job Coach Wooden had wanted all along, and it was his for the taking. Many people would say that he should have simply called UCLA back and said he had reconsidered. After all, he had not signed a contract. There was nothing in writing. Would it be so wrong to tell UCLA he had changed his mind?

But for John Wooden, that would be unthinkable. He had given his word, and his word was his bond. He would not go back on it. Coach Wooden believes that by maintaining his integrity and keeping his word to UCLA, he allowed God to lead his life in a direction he would not have chosen for himself. That direction turned out far better than he would have imagined. And God used a Minnesota ice storm (plus John Wooden's integrity) to achieve that purpose in his life.

> *Ability may get you to the top, but it takes character to keep you there.*

Coach later reflected, "If fate had not intervened, I would never have gone to UCLA. But my dad's little set of threes served me well: 'Don't whine. Don't complain. Don't make excuses.' . . . Things turn out best for those who make the best of the way things turn out."[5]

Coach also built a shelter against a rainy day through his character trait of diligence—a strong work ethic—which his father taught him. "You had to work hard [on the farm]," Coach recalled. "Dad felt there was time for play, but always after the chores and the studies were done." He and his brother got up hours before school started to do their chores around the farm. When they returned home from school, they had more chores to do, then it was time for homework in the evening. So John Wooden grew up accepting hard work as the norm in life. He carried that attitude into his playing days in high school and college. "I couldn't do much about my height," he said, "but I could do something about my condition. I always wanted to be in the best possible condition, and I hoped that others wouldn't work as hard at it as I did."

The willingness to work harder than your competition is more important than talent, intelligence, and luck in determining your level of success. People who work hard are unusual in our culture, and they generally achieve unusual levels of success. The grades you earned in school are often less important than the effort you expended to get those grades. I've found that people who work their tails off to get a C+ or B– usually achieve greater success in life than those who can effortlessly coast to an A.

Ray Alba was already playing at UCLA when Coach Wooden arrived in 1948. He recalled that Coach's arrival marked a dramatic change in the atmosphere on the team. Suddenly, the old relaxed and easygoing atmosphere was gone. Coach Wooden demanded hard work. His practices were rigorous and exhausting. "At first," Alba said, "I was angry and said, 'What the heck is this guy doing?'" Coach insisted on strict adherence to team rules, and Alba was nearly thrown off the team when he was caught in a bar one night after bed check. Coach decided to give Alba another chance, he recalled, "and from then on, I made all my bed checks."

Alba looks back with gratitude on the values and work ethic he absorbed from Coach. "I learned from John Wooden," he said, "that it takes hard work and perseverance to get what you're going after. Success is a lot of hard work. It isn't something magical that comes along. It's not a matter of a lucky break. It's you working for the break and working very hard."

Another John Wooden character trait is persistence. Roland Underhill played for Coach in the 1950s, and he reminded me that, even though Coach achieved a big turnaround as soon as he arrived in 1948, it actually took him sixteen years to achieve a national championship at UCLA. "Coach kept at it," Underhill said, "and never stopped persevering. He didn't change his style, but he kept honing his craft. And in all of those years, Coach never compromised his values."

It's not so important who starts the game but who finishes it.

As the late football coach George Allen once observed, "People of mediocre ability sometimes achieve outstanding success because they don't know when to quit. Most men succeed because they are determined to."[6] The determination to persevere against obstacles and opposition all the way to a goal is a strong shelter against the rainy days of tough circumstances and harsh criticism. When the rainy seasons of life come, let persistence and perseverance shelter you and carry you through to success.

A Shelter of Self-Discipline

One of the most important virtues Joshua Hugh Wooden taught his four sons was self-discipline. He taught them, first of all, to be disciplined in their speech, and he was a role model of disciplined speech. Coach said of his father, "I never heard him speak an ill word of anybody. I never heard him use a word of profanity."

Joshua Hugh Wooden also taught his sons self-discipline by imposing discipline on them. Coach recalled a time when he and his brother Maurice were in the barn, cleaning out adjoining horse stalls. Maurice was in one stall, John in the other.

"This brother was three years older than I," Coach said, "and he had a pitchfork of manure that he threw right over into my face. I was irritated. Considerably. I couldn't whip him because he was three years older and I knew I couldn't, but I didn't think about that. I went after him. But the thing I did so poorly was I called him a name that I shouldn't have called him. My dad happened to overhear and Dad took action and I had the hardest whipping I ever received. I think my brother got a harder one. I don't think to this day anyone has heard me use a word of profanity since. . . . We all need lessons of that sort occasionally. Self-control is so important in whatever you are doing."[7]

In all the interviews I have conducted with literally hundreds of people who know Coach Wooden, I haven't found one person who heard him say anything stronger than, "Goodness gracious sakes alive"—and he only says that when he's *really* upset!

Duffy Daugherty was head football coach of the Michigan State Spartans from 1954 to 1972. During a road game against UCLA, the score was tied at 14 with only seconds left in regulation play. So Daugherty sent in his kicker, Dave Kaiser, to kick the field goal. The ball was snapped, and Kaiser kicked it toward the end zone, but Coach Daugherty noticed that Kaiser wasn't even watching the ball. He was looking at ground level, toward the officials. The ball sailed through the uprights. Michigan State won, 17–14.

As Kaiser returned to the sidelines, his teammates went wild. Daugherty hugged him and shouted, "Nice going, Dave, but why didn't you watch the ball after you kicked it?"

"I couldn't see it," Kaiser said. "I forgot my contact lenses at the hotel, so I had to watch the officials to know if the kick was good or not. Coach, I couldn't even see the goalposts!"

For a moment, Daugherty was angry because Dave Kaiser hadn't informed him he didn't have his contact lenses. Had Coach Daugherty known, he probably would have made a different decision.

But after a moment's reflection, he realized that Kaiser had kicked the ball perfectly and confidently because he was a supremely disciplined kicker. After making that kick hundreds of times in practice, his body knew the angle and distance to the goal. He didn't need to see the ball. Discipline alone enabled him to kick the game-winning field goal.[8]

While I was writing this book, I had a chat with football coach Howard Schnellenberger, who has spent more than half a century coaching at the college level and in the NFL. He was on Don Shula's staff during the heyday of the Miami Dolphins. I asked Howard for his impression of Shula as a leader. "Don Shula is the most organized and disciplined person I've ever met," he told me. "Every date on his monthly planner was blocked out a month in advance. He could look at his planner and tell you exactly what he'd be doing at least thirty days out. Those dogged organizational skills allowed Shula to remain at a high performance level on a consistent basis. Coach Shula was disciplined and dedicated. I've worked under some of the greatest coaches in the game—Shula, Bear Bryant, George Allen, Blanton Collier—and the common denominator among these coaches was that they were all extremely disciplined and totally dedicated to their profession. Inordinately so."

We all admire disciplined people, but few of us want to devote time and effort to disciplining ourselves. Yet people who are truly self-disciplined have their own shelter already built when the rainy days come.

Recently I had a dental issue that had to be taken care of, by far the most complicated and physically taxing dental procedure I've ever had. It involved an extraction, an implant, a later visit for a crown, and so forth. My dentist could see that I was feeling nervous and concerned about it. She said, "The first visit will take about an hour. All the exercise you do and the way you've always watched your diet will help you get through this. You'll have no trouble at all." She was telling me that I had built a shelter against the rainy day when I would have this procedure done.

Those who have taken the time to practice the physical disciplines of good exercise and good nutrition are the best prepared to deal with the rainy day of an accident or an illness—or a major dental procedure. Those who are spiritually disciplined, who have regular habits of prayer and Scripture study, are best prepared to deal with the rainy day of a spiritual crisis. And those who are financially disciplined are far better equipped to deal with economic hard times than those who are not.

Have you built a shelter against a rainy day by the disciplined way you live your financial life? Here is some practical counsel to consider.

1. *Beware the warning signs of out-of-control finances*, such as an inability to pay your monthly bills on time, an inability to save money on a regular basis, an inability to pay more than the minimum payments on your credit cards, credit cards that are maxed out, frequent attempts to borrow your way out of debt, and frequent arguments with your husband or wife over money.

2. *Stay out of debt.* If you are already in debt, learn to live within your means, pay off your debts, and begin building net worth. Before John and Nell Wooden were married in 1932, he saved up $900 to get their marriage off to a good

start. Just days before their wedding day, the First Bank and Trust Company (where he had his savings account) failed. In those pre-FDIC days, there was no insurance for his savings account. The money was simply gone. The father of Nell's best friend offered John a $200 loan so they could get married and start their life together. John was reluctant to take the money, but he finally accepted the loan. He paid the money back as soon as he was able and vowed never to borrow money again, except to take out a mortgage on a home.

3. *Start a rainy-day fund.* Set aside money for emergencies. Keep it in a safe, interest-bearing account, not in stocks, which might lose value. A good rule of thumb is to maintain a fund equal to six months' worth of expenses. So if you spend $5,000 a month on necessities, set aside at least $30,000 in your rainy-day fund.

4. *Invest for the future.* Accumulate savings for your retirement, children's college fund, vacation of a lifetime, or other big financial goals. Learn about the "miracle of compounding."[9] Albert Einstein once said, "Compounding is mankind's greatest invention because it allows for the reliable, systematic accumulation of wealth. The eighth wonder of the world is the miracle of compounding." Thanks to compound interest, a young person age twenty to twenty-five can become a millionaire by retirement age with nothing more than a decent job and a measure of self-discipline.

A Shelter of Faith

But Joshua Hugh Wooden was not thinking primarily of money when he told his sons to build a shelter against a rainy day. Faith, Coach once said, "is the greatest shelter of all. In many ways we've been taken in by materialism. I'm not saying possessions are unimportant, but we often put them out of proportion, ahead of family, faith, and friends."[10]

Swen Nater told me that the sixth principle is a profoundly *spiritual* principle. "Coach would tell you this is not necessarily a question of saving your money," he said. "It means doing things in advance in anticipation of those rocky days that are inevitable. Be good to people, and they will be there to help you. Build your knowledge through good books. Have the discipline to take care of your health. Above all, develop faith and patience. They were two big ones for John Wooden."

Coach Wooden has always practiced a quiet but radiant kind of faith. He does not press his beliefs on other people, but he gently shares his convictions in a way that makes others want to know more. "It is my belief," he once wrote, "that in one way or another we are all seeking success. And success is peace of mind, a direct result of self-satisfaction in knowing that you did your best to become the best that you are capable of becoming, and not just in a physical way. 'Seek ye first His kingdom and His righteousness and all these things will be yours as well.'"[11] That last line is a quotation from Jesus in Matthew 6:33 (KJV).

Coach's favorite Scripture passage is the thirteenth chapter of 1 Corinthians, which contains these words:

> Love is patient, love is kind. It does not envy, it does not boast, it is not proud. It is not rude, it is not self-seeking, it is not easily angered, it keeps no record of wrongs. Love does not delight in evil but rejoices with the truth. It always protects, always trusts, always hopes, always perseveres.
> Love never fails.
>
> verses 4–8 NIV

Coach often said, "Love is the most important word in the English language, followed by balance. Achieving love and balance isn't hard if that's where you put your priorities."[12]

Former UCLA player Brad Holland told me that Coach Wooden truly lives out the sixth principle of his father's seven-point creed. "With Coach," he said, "building a shelter against a rainy day is something you do every day by the way you maintain your relationships, by the way you treat the people around you, by the way you talk to God and listen to his Word. You have to begin building that shelter in your youth and keep building it every day of your life. What will you lean on when the rainy days hit? Will you lean on money or possessions or fame or some other idol? Or will you lean on God? Coach Wooden has built a shelter that will stand firm when the rains come. That's why he's such a role model for us all."

A Shelter of Friends

Our friends are another shelter against a rainy day. We all need the shelter of people who will be close to us and available to us throughout our lives, in both the good times and the tough times. In "Rainy Day People," songwriter Gordon Lightfoot sings about friends who seem to show up exactly when you need them most. They don't feel they have to fill the silence with talk. They "just listen till they've heard it all."

To have rainy-day people in your life, you must be a rainy-day friend to others. Whenever you reach out to people who are going through tough times, you accumulate a store of friendship and goodwill that will eventually flow back to you in your own time of need. Many coaches have admirers, but Coach Wooden has hundreds of *friends* who would give him the shirt off their backs. He has many rainy-day people in his life because he's been such a good rainy-day friend to others.

Steve Lavin was UCLA head basketball coach from 1996 to 2003. During his time at UCLA, he received many encouraging notes from Coach Wooden. "When I was having trouble at UCLA," Steve told me, "Coach Wooden would write me the most thoughtful letters. Sometimes he'd write me about the importance of integrity. When we lost a tough game, he wrote me about the criticism he received whenever he would lose a game."

Steve Fisher, who now coaches at San Diego State, was an assistant and later head coach at Michigan from 1982 to 1997. He told me, "In 1993, we lost to North Carolina in the NCAA Finals. That was the so-called 'Timeout Game,' which haunts Chris Webber to this day." In that game, Webber called a time-out with eleven seconds left to play and with Michigan trailing 73–71, but Michigan had no time-outs remaining. Because of that mistake, Webber was called for a technical foul, which sealed Michigan's fate.

"Chris was a finalist for the John Wooden Award," Fisher explained, "and had agreed to go to Los Angeles for the ceremony. But after his mistake in that final game, he knew he wouldn't win and didn't want to go. But his father and I convinced him to go, so he went. The day before the dinner there was a little luncheon, and Coach Wooden attended. He knew what Chris was going through and saw that the young man was really down, so he took him aside in a private room and gave him a pep talk.

"Thirty minutes later, Chris came out with a smile on his face. Coach had talked to him, signed a *Pyramid of Success* for him, and absolutely lifted his spirits. All the way home, Chris thanked me and told me how much meeting John Wooden had meant to him. Chris will never forget that act of kindness, and neither will I."

Mike Tschirret, a former high school coach in Florida, told me about a 1974 trip he made to the Final Four in Greensboro, North Carolina. Mike was having breakfast with several fellow high school coaches on the morning of the semifinals, in which UCLA would be playing. The coaches heard a voice behind them say, "Do you mind if an old man joins you?" They all looked up and saw John Wooden approaching their table.

145

"We ended up talking with him for about ninety minutes," Tschirret recalled. "We talked about basketball, life in general, religion, all sorts of things. At one point I asked, 'Coach, don't you have anything better to do than talk to a bunch of high school coaches? You've got a big game today.' He just smiled at us and said, 'I can't think of anything I'd rather do.'"

Former UCLA sports information director Bill Bennett shares the same birthday with Coach, and they always call each other every October 14 to exchange birthday greetings. Bill once told me, "Last year, I got to the office especially early because I wanted to be the first one to leave a happy birthday message. But when I got to my desk, I saw that I already had a message. Of course, it was from Coach Wooden! He had beaten me to the punch. I saved that message, and every day I start my morning by listening to Coach Wooden singing 'Happy Birthday' to me."

Gary Cunningham, who was a UCLA assistant coach under John Wooden, recalled, "Coach Wooden was a great friend and mentor to me and to everyone who worked for him and played for him. I had lunch recently with [former Bruin player] Lynn Shackleford, and he told me that Coach was the most influential person in his life. I can't help thinking that what Coach has been to all of us, his father was to him.

"The amazing thing is that Coach has actually done more good and touched more lives since his retirement in 1975 than he did in his entire coaching career. I often ask former UCLA players why they have breakfast with Coach at VIP'S. They say to me, 'He's fun to be with.' And it's true. He is. But there's more to it than that. A lot more. When you spend time around Coach, you come away a different person. A better person."

Many people who know Coach remark about his amazing ability to remember names. Seth Greenberg, head basketball coach of the Virginia Tech Hokies, told me that he once encountered Coach Wooden at an airport. Greenberg's wife,

Karen, and two-year-old daughter, Paige, were with him, and he introduced them to Coach. About two years later, Karen Greenberg went to the airport to pick Seth up, and there was Coach Wooden, sitting alone on a bench. She went over and greeted him, and Coach recognized her instantly and asked, "How is your daughter Paige?" Another three years passed, and Seth and Karen Greenberg encountered Coach Wooden at a coaches retreat, and again Coach recognized Karen, greeted her by name, and asked how her daughter Paige was.

Seth Greenberg said, "I was amazed. I thought, 'How does he do that?' Then it hit me: Coach takes the time to listen and hear, which is a lost art. Coach talks *with* people and *to* people, not at them."

Again and again, Coach Wooden has gone out of his way to be a friend to others, on both sunny days and rainy days. And when the rain fell in his own life, when his wife, Nell, passed away and his sorrow was almost more than he could bear, he had many, many friends who loved him, reached out to him, and prayed for him in his loss. As broadcaster Dick Enberg told me, "He lamented her loss for a long time, and for a while it seemed he had lost his desire to live. His family and friends cared for him and helped him recover."

A Shelter of Family

Coach Wooden's family has always been a shelter in his life. Former college coach George Terzian recalled a conference game he attended, when the Bruins lost because their opponent held the ball. "After Coach met with his team," Terzian said, "he came out onto the floor to greet his family and friends. I was amazed at the look of real joy on his face as he hugged his grandchildren. You would never have known he had just lost an important conference game under exasperating circumstances."

John Wooden married his high school sweetheart. She was, in fact, the only girl John Wooden ever dated. Their romance got off to a slow start. He was a freshman at Martinsville High School, and he noticed Nell Riley around the campus. Although he was attracted to her, he later said, "I didn't think she'd give sour apples for me, a farm boy who was extremely shy."

Fortunately for John Wooden, Nell wasn't shy at all. One hot summer day, she asked her best friend Mary to have her brother Jack drive them out by the Wooden farm. They stopped by the side of the road and saw Johnny behind a mule, plowing in the field, his skin caked with dust and dripping with sweat. Nell called to him and waved, but John kept plowing, ignoring her. Finally, they drove away.

In the fall, when school started, Nell cornered John Wooden in the hallway. She asked, "Why were you so rude to me when Mary and I went out to see you at the farm?"

John stammered nervously, "I was dirty and sweaty, and I thought you'd probably make fun of me."

Nell smiled sweetly. "Johnny," she said, "I would never make fun of you. Ever."

Coach later recalled, "Something happened in me right then. That spark has never gone away."

From then on, John and Nell were inseparable. They walked to school and back each day. They went to the Grace Theatre to see the latest Charlie Chaplin comedy or Tom Mix western and often stopped by Shireman's Ice Cream Parlor or Wick's Candy Kitchen for something sweet. Then Johnny and Nell would sit together in the Riley family's porch swing, holding hands.

Nell joined the pep band, not because she had any great musical talent (her friends accused her of faking her cornet playing) but so that she would have a courtside seat for all of Johnny's games. During those high school games, John and Nellie began a ritual that continued throughout his playing and coaching career. During the pregame huddle, John would position himself so he could see Nell in the stands. As they made eye contact, she would smile and give him an okay sign with her thumb and forefinger, and he would wink back at her. That ritual, he recalled, "carried right through to the last game I ever coached."

How did John Wooden propose to Nell Riley? He didn't! "We simply agreed during my senior year that when I finished college we'd see the preacher," he explained. "Nell and I were together through everything that followed—high school, college, family, friends, and my life teaching and coaching. She is the greatest thing that ever happened to me."[13]

Once, when someone asked Coach to name his top priorities in life, he said, "Faith, family, and friends." Then, after a pause, he added, "Sometimes I put family first. That's not really the proper order, but I think the Lord understands."

Through his words and his life, Coach teaches us the truth of his father's creed: Build a shelter against a rainy day by the life you live—and you will never have to fear the storms of tomorrow.

8

Pray for Guidance and Counsel, and Give Thanks for Your Blessings Each Day

John Wooden and Nell Riley were baptized together in 1927, when they were juniors in high school. "She suggested that we join [the church] at the same time," Coach recalled. "I don't want to say that I accepted Christ at that particular time because of the fact that I did this primarily because she wanted me to. But my acceptance came gradually as time went by."[1]

When Coach and I compared notes on our spiritual experiences, he said, "I know that when some people make a decision for Christ, everything instantly changes in their lives. But for me, there was not one specific day or hour when I committed my life to Christ. My experience with the Lord was gradual. But I do remember coming to a point as a young man where I looked back and realized that I had been a believer for quite some time.

"I've trusted Christ, and I've tried to live as he would have me live. I've studied his Word, and I've prayed a great deal. I have faith that he will do what he's promised. I'm ready to meet him, and I'm anxious to see Nellie, but all in due time. I don't want to outlive my children or my grandchildren, but neither am I anxious to leave my family. Actually, I've put all that into God's hands."

When John Wooden joined the navy, he took with him a small metal cross that his pastor had given him. He had orders to ship out to the Pacific aboard the carrier USS *Franklin* (CV-13). He took a short leave in Indiana and was on his way to preflight in Iowa City when he experienced severe abdominal pains. He tried to ignore the pain but finally saw a navy doctor who told him he had a red-hot appendix and needed an emergency appendectomy. The surgery kept him Stateside, and a buddy of his from Purdue, Freddie Stalcup, took his place aboard the *Franklin*.

On March 19, 1945, while the *Franklin* was within fifty miles of the Japanese mainland, carrying out airstrikes against targets on shore, Japanese bombers and kamikaze aircraft attacked the ship. Freddie Stalcup was at his battle station, manning the antiaircraft guns, when he was killed by a kamikaze attack. He was one of 724 American sailors who died aboard the *Franklin* that day. Only the incredible heroism of the surviving crew members kept the critically wounded carrier from sinking.

John Wooden often wondered why his life was saved by an inflamed appendix, and why his friend and fraternity brother, Freddie Stalcup, died instead. "But for the emergency appendectomy that seemed so unfortunate when it happened," he reflected, "John Wooden's name rather than Freddie Stalcup's would probably have been on the casualty list."[2]

When I first heard this story, I was reminded of the words of Jesus in John 15:13: "Greater love has no one than this, that one lay down his life for his friends" (NIV). In a very real sense, Freddie died in place of John Wooden. When Coach recounts that story, I hear gratitude in his words—gratitude to God for sparing his life and gratitude to Freddie for dying in his place and dying for his country.

After recovering from his surgery, John Wooden served in the navy as a physical conditioning instructor from 1943 to 1946, rising to the rank of lieutenant. He always kept the metal cross in his pocket, not as a good-luck charm but as a simple reminder of God's presence in his life.

Even in civilian life, he kept the cross with him at all times. It served as a reminder to keep him humble during his record-setting winning streaks at UCLA—and to keep him centered when his team was struggling. Just taking a moment to reflect on the meaning of that cross, he said, gave him a sense of peace. That cross was in his pocket during every Bruins game he coached, and Nell kept a matching cross in her purse.

An Attitude of Gratitude

The life of Coach John Wooden is marked by gratitude. He continually expresses thanks to God and to other people. If he receives a letter from a fan, he replies with a note in his own hand that typically begins, "Many thanks for your kind note. . . ."

I believe Coach Wooden's attitude of gratitude has a lot to do with his long and successful life. When you are thankful for your blessings, more blessings flow your way. Studies show that people who express gratitude to God and to others on a regular basis generally experience a more optimistic mood, are less subject to depression, and are less prone to the many physical problems that often result from stress. Gratitude is good medicine.

"Give thanks for your blessings and pray for guidance every day," Joshua Hugh Wooden told his son Johnny in the final principle of his seven-point creed. Reflecting on this principle, Coach himself wrote, "So often we fail to acknowledge what we have because we're so concerned about what we want.

> *It's the little details that are vital. Little things make big things happen.*

We fail to give real thanks for the many blessings for which we did nothing: our life itself, the flowers, the trees, our family and friends. This moment. All of our blessings we take for granted so much of the time."[3]

His words remind me of the counsel of the medieval monk Thomas à Kempis, who wrote, "Be thankful for the smallest blessing, and you will deserve to receive greater. Value the least gifts no less than the greatest, and the simple graces as especial favors. If you remember the dignity of the Giver, no gift will seem small or mean."[4]

Coach always expresses gratitude for even the smallest of favors. For example, I've heard from several people that when they've been at a restaurant with Coach and the waitress comes by to fill the water glasses, everyone at the table ignores the waitress except Coach. He will invariably stop in midsentence, smile at the waitress, and say, "Thank you." It's not a big deal, but in our society, it's a rare thing to acknowledge and thank the wait staff at a restaurant.

An attitude of gratitude begins with a sense of humility. Arrogant people are incapable of gratitude. Coach Wooden's sense of gratitude begins with his deep humility and his unconditional love for people. As educator Anne Husted Burleigh once observed, "Gratitude, like love, is not a feeling but an act of the will. We choose to be thankful just as we choose to love."[5]

In choosing to be thankful in every circumstance in life, Coach seems to intuitively understand a principle so many of us miss: Gratitude is the key to happiness. Grateful people are happy people. They learn to look for pleasure in simple blessings. They find something to be grateful for even when things don't go their way. They focus on what they *have* instead of what they *want*.

Count Your Blessings

Coach Wooden's attitude of gratitude is infectious. Dustin Kerns, a young assistant coach at Santa Clara University, told me, "Coach Wooden gave me the seven-point creed, and I carry it in my wallet every day. The seventh principle is so important: 'Give thanks for your blessings and pray for guidance every day.' I'm thankful for all the opportunities I've received as a college coach. I tell my players to be thankful for a free education and the chance to play Division I basketball. I remind them to be grateful every day for all the blessings they have in life."

And former Bruins player Brad Holland said, "The seventh creed captures John Wooden and his optimism about life. He always feels that God has truly blessed him, and he speaks of how fortunate he has been to have a loving family and wonderful players to coach. John Wooden knows where he came from and that God put him in a position to leave an impact on literally thousands of young lives. He has truly taught me what it means to be grateful for life's blessings."

The old saying "Count your blessings" may sound like Pollyanna advice. But it's actually a realistic way to realign your emotions and balance your thinking so that your highs don't get too high nor your lows too low. Some people feel entitled to be wealthy, successful, and victorious all the time, and when things don't go their way, they become bitter, angry, and depressed. But when you view the good things in your life as blessings rather than as entitlements, you can feel grateful

155

for those blessings without going into an emotional nosedive when times are tough. A grateful attitude will keep you on an emotional even keel. Here, then, are some suggestions for living a lifestyle of counting your blessings every day.

1. *Keep a gratitude journal.* For a limited period of time—say, four to six weeks—keep a journal in which you record all the events and people you feel grateful for. The reason you need to keep this journal only for a limited time is that its purpose is to retrain your thinking. Once you have kept a gratitude journal for a period of weeks, you'll begin to see blessings in every circumstance, even in challenging times. Your mind will be reoriented to focus on the positive instead of the negative. Later, if you notice you are losing your thankful mind-set, simply go back and reread your gratitude journal or begin keeping a gratitude journal again for a while.

2. *Practice saying thank you.* Every day, there are people who do things for you, who make your life a little bit easier or more pleasant. Most of the time, we don't even notice these people. If we would make a habit of saying thank you—and *meaning* it—every time someone serves us in some way, it would make a huge difference in our attitude. Author Melody Beattie writes:

> Gratitude unlocks the fullness of life. It turns what we have into enough, and more. It turns denial into acceptance, chaos to order, confusion to clarity. It can turn a meal into a feast, a house into a home, a stranger into a friend. It turns problems into gifts, failures into successes, the unexpected into perfect timing, and mistakes into important events. It can turn an existence into a real life, and disconnected situations into important and beneficial lessons. Gratitude makes sense of our past, brings peace for today, and creates a vision for tomorrow.
>
> Gratitude makes things right. . . . Say thank you until you mean it. If you say it long enough, you will believe it.[6]

So thank the mailman and the newspaper boy. Thank the clerk at the grocery store. Astonish your boss by going into his office and thanking him for your job. If *you* are the boss, then thank your employees for working hard to make your business successful. Thank your doctor and nurse for giving you a checkup and looking after your health. Write a letter and thank your elected representatives when they do something you approve of. (Give them enough praise, and they just might keep up the good work!)

3. *Send thank-you notes.* Purchase a quantity of thank-you cards and stamps, and always have them ready to send out to people. Get in the habit of writing handwritten notes to people who show you some kindness or send you a letter. Emails are fast but make a shallow impression. A handwritten note makes a much deeper impression because personalized gratitude is becoming a lost art. Think of the impression it makes on you to receive a real card, inscribed in ink in actual handwriting, sent to your home with a real postage stamp. That is an act of rare grace these days—and because it's so uncommon, it shows how much you care.

4. *Use gratitude and praise to build people up.* Investor-philanthropist Warren Buffett, CEO of Berkshire Hathaway, has a rule he follows in his dealings with his employees: "Praise by name, criticize by category." If an individual in his organization is performing poorly, he doesn't single that person out for blame or humiliation; he criticizes the category or division of his company that is not performing well. But if an individual makes an outstanding contribution to the company, he singles that person out for praise and thanks. He always builds people up; he never tears them down.

I flew to Cincinnati in February 2010, and a driver named Bob Ward met me at the airport. At the end of my stay, Bob drove me back to the airport. Along the way, I asked him who were some of the memorable people he had driven in his limo.

"One of the most memorable," he said without hesitating, "was General Colin Powell. He arrived at a small airport here in Cincinnati in a private plane. As he got into my car, he said, 'Before we go to the hotel, I need to make a stop at a place called the Sherman House.' I had never heard of it, so I called my dispatcher for help in finding the place. The dispatcher said, 'Oh, it's in a very bad neighborhood.'

"Well, I found the location. When we arrived, I discovered that it's a home for homeless military veterans. I went in with General Powell, and he spoke for about twenty minutes to the men who lived there. He got them laughing and showed them a real good time, and he also thanked them for their service. I could tell it had been a long time since a lot of those guys had ever heard one of their countrymen say, 'Thank you.'

"After that, I took him to his hotel. General Powell was in Cincinnati to give a corporate speech—that was the primary reason for his trip. But I think his service of kindness and saying thank you to those homeless vets was his most important mission."

Then Bob Ward told me a story about someone else he had driven in his limo. "I had Senator Robert Dole in my car one time," he said. "Senator Dole was very interested in what I thought about the issues affecting the country. I guess that's how he kept in touch with what average people are thinking. He asked me some questions, and he was genuinely focused on what I told him.

"When we got to the airport, I said, 'Senator Dole, I just want to thank you for all the contributions you have made to this country. You're a great American, and I am proud to have met you.' Well, Mr. Dole got very emotional. I thought he was going to cry. He said, 'Rarely do I ever hear anyone say that to me. You have encouraged me greatly.'" That's the power of a few simple words of gratitude to reach the human heart and build people up.

In January 2010, ESPN aired a TV show about Peyton Manning, who had just been named Most Valuable Player of the NFL. The story told about something Peyton Manning has been quietly doing for years. Whenever opponents he admires retire from their football careers, Manning writes a handwritten note to them, congratulating them on their careers and thanking them for their character and for being the kind of people they are. ESPN learned of these notes and interviewed some of the recipients. The players all expressed their appreciation for this act of gratitude and kindness from one of the greatest quarterbacks of all time.

Vince Dooley, the longtime head football coach and athletic director at the University of Georgia, expressed what it feels like to be on the receiving end of someone's gratitude. In his book *Dooley: My Forty Years at Georgia*, he writes:

> I've always said that the great thing about being a teacher or a coach is that you continue to enjoy it for the rest of your life through your players and students. All the memories of competition don't become less important, but what becomes increasingly more important are the players who come back and say two simple words: "Thanks, Coach."
>
> Some thank me for teaching them the simple lessons of discipline. Or they're grateful because I taught them to win—and to lose—with dignity and class. Or I taught them the work ethic that they would take with them and use for the rest of their lives. Or I taught them how to work through adversity in order to achieve their goals.
>
> That's because the teachers you always remember are the ones who are the most demanding. . . . When someone like Billy Payne, who has accomplished so much since his days at Georgia, expresses his appreciation, that is something I just can't put a value on.[7]

The beautiful thing about gratitude is that it does so much good for those who give it—and for those who receive it. So be thankful for the blessings that come your way. Be thankful to God and thankful to other people.

It All Comes Down to Prayer

Swen Nater told me, "John Wooden is a man of prayer. One time, while I was job hunting, I went to Coach for advice. He said, 'Swen, would you like me to pray about this with you? Let's ask God for his guidance in your life.' I never forgot that. He always honored God and his Word. Talking to God was as natural to Coach as talking to his wife and kids. He didn't hesitate to say, 'How can I pray for you?' or 'Why don't we pray about this right now?' He knew that none of us can make it through life without God."

The seventh principle of Joshua Hugh Wooden's seven-point creed is actually a two-part principle. The first half is, "Pray for guidance and counsel . . ." The second half is ". . . and give thanks for your blessings each day."

As Coach himself wrote, "One of my players at UCLA once told me he was embarrassed to have anyone know that he prayed. There's no shame in praying for guidance. It's a sign of strength."[8]

Those who played for Coach and worked alongside him say they are continually impressed by the way he lives out his faith. His walk with God is a fully integrated and natural dimension of his life. Coach's relationship with God defines who he is.

Fred Hessler, longtime UCLA radio announcer, said, "John Wooden tried harder than any man I have ever met to be like Jesus Christ." And Los Angeles sportswriter Bud Furillo observed, "John Wooden proves that Christian ideals must work. They do in his life." And longtime UCLA golf coach Eddie Merrins said, "Coach doesn't wear his faith on his sleeve, but everything he does in life is designed to please God."

Jamaal Wilkes agrees that Coach Wooden isn't one to push his faith on anyone else. Yet he is so easygoing and comfortable with his faith that he will readily talk to you about God or pray with you, if that's what you want and need. "Coach didn't spend a lot of time preaching to us about God," Jamaal told me, "but his actions always speak louder than his words. I was with him every day for three years at UCLA and never heard him swear. He's intense and competitive, but he always maintains his self-control. I think that's because his life is truly controlled by God. He trusts that God is in control of all of his circumstances. Coach never wastes time worrying about things he can't control. He knows that God already has everything handled. His attitude is, 'Keep the faith—and the faith will keep you.'"

Jay Carty told me, "Coach has always been a believer in Christ, but he's never been on a soapbox about his beliefs. As a coach at a public university, he didn't feel that would be appropriate. But as we wrote our two books together, it was exciting and rewarding to see Coach share his heart for God. John Wooden is a man of prayer. If you spend any time around him at all, you quickly discover that this is a man who has a close communion with the Lord."

Bill Bennett, longtime UCLA sports information director, told me about the role of faith and prayer in Coach Wooden's life: "Coach has a simple childlike faith," he said. "I wouldn't call him a Bible scholar or an evangelist. He just trusts the Lord totally for all his earthly needs. He doesn't worry and fret over issues because he knows that God will work it all out in his time. It's a beautiful thing to watch this great man and the special relationship he has with his God. It's a wonderful approach to life that we all should emulate. It all comes down to prayer. I've always believed John Wooden and the Lord have this special union that you don't see very often. I just feel Coach has a direct pipeline to God. They communicate very clearly and directly to each other."

It's a beautiful thing to see a coach who cares not only about the mental and physical conditioning of his players but also about their spiritual condition. I've known a number of coaches who truly love their players enough to pray *for* them and pray *with* them.

My friend Jay Strack, who conducted the wedding ceremony for my wife, Ruth, and me, has conducted many chapel services for professional sports teams. A few years ago, when Tony Dungy was head coach of the Tampa Bay Buccaneers, the organization asked Jay to conduct a pregame chapel for the Bucs. Jay arrived early at the facility and located the room where the chapel would take place. There he found a man at work, setting up chairs.

Jay walked into the room and said, "Hi, I'm Jay Strack."

The man turned around, and Jay recognized him as Coach Dungy. "Hi, I'm Tony Dungy," he said.

"Coach," Jay said, "I'm here to lead the chapel. Let me help you set up these chairs."

"No thanks," Coach Dungy said. "I like to set up each chair myself. I know where each man sits. I know his needs and where he's hurting. I pray over each man's chair as I set it up."

Now, that is a coach after John Wooden's own heart. That is a coach who lives and breathes prayer.

Dominated by Love

There's a simple three-line formula that Coach Wooden loves to quote. No one knows who penned these lines, but they truly express the heart and the life of John Wooden:

> Talent is God-given: be humble.
> Fame is man-given: be thankful.
> Conceit is self-given: be careful.

Coach's humble spirit and his grateful attitude are truly rooted in his faith in God.

Steve Jamison, John Wooden's longtime writing partner, told me about a conversation he had with Coach about God. "In December 2009," Steve said, "I had breakfast with Coach at VIP'S. I asked him questions about his religion. I asked, 'What does heaven look like?' He said, 'I don't know.' Then I asked, 'What does God look like?' He said, 'I don't know, but I know he is real.' That said it all to me. A simple childlike belief in God—no great argument or debate. His attitude was, 'This is what I believe, and I'm not wavering.' Coach knows that Nell is in heaven and he will join her immediately upon his death. He's rock solid on that. And that's why he lives each day with such peace and assurance."

In his book *They Call Me Coach*, John Wooden tells a story about another coach from a bygone era, Amos Alonzo Stagg. Though Coach Stagg was known primarily as a college football coach, he was also influential in developing the sport of basketball, and he played in the first public basketball game at the Springfield, Massachusetts, YMCA on March 11, 1892. He is also credited with the invention of the batting cage in the game of baseball. He spent most of his coaching career at the University of Chicago and the College of the Pacific in Stockton, California. He continued coaching well into his nineties and died in Stockton at age 102.

As Coach Wooden tells the story, Coach Stagg was once asked why he coached long after most people would retire and take life easy. Stagg replied that he coached because he had made a promise to God. "As a young man," Coach Wooden writes, "Stagg planned to become a minister and attended Yale Theological School. One day after talking with God through prayer he decided he could best serve Him on the athletic field rather than from the pulpit."

Stagg explained his decision in these words: "I have made the young men of America my ministry. I have tried to bring out the best in the boys that I have coached. I truly believe that many of them have become better Christians and citizens because of what they have learned on the athletic field."

Finally, Coach Wooden quotes a statement by Amos Alonzo Stagg that truly expresses Coach's own heart: "You must love your boys to get the most out of them and do the most for them. I have worked with boys whom I haven't admired, but I have loved them just the same. Love has dominated my coaching career as I'm sure it has and always will that of many other coaches and teachers."[9]

> *If you're not making mistakes, then you're not doing anything. I'm positive that a doer makes mistakes.*

Coach Wooden once wrote about the faith that has guided him throughout his life and career. Faith, he wrote, "cannot be acquired without prayer. . . . Faith is not just waiting, hoping, and wanting things to happen. Rather it is working hard to make things happen and realizing that there are no failures—just disappointments—when you have done your best. As someone once said, 'If you do your best, angels can do no better.'"[10]

Joshua Hugh Wooden would be very proud of the life his son Johnny has lived—a life shaped by faith, by love, and by a simple seven-point creed. Johnny has always done his best. Angels could do no better.

Epilogue

hen word came of Coach John Wooden's passing, I knew I had to be at the memorial service on June 26, 2010. So I called the ever-efficient Bill Bennett at UCLA, and he helped make the arrangements for me. The UCLA Athletic Department was very gracious and made a place for me in the reserved seating section.

I called my friend Ken Wilson of Ken Wilson Media Services in Los Angeles. For many years, he has been my tour guide whenever I have been in L.A. to promote a book. Ken had known Coach Wooden and had driven him to various events over the years, so Ken and I had a shared sense of loss. I flew from Orlando to L.A. on Friday, and Ken picked me up at the Airport Marriott at nine o'clock on Saturday morning. We arrived at the UCLA campus at about ten and walked under gloomy leaden skies toward Pauley Pavilion.

Crossing Bruin Plaza, we came upon the life-size Bruin statue, looking as huge and fierce as a living California grizzly. Arranged around the base of the statue were flowers, balloons, notes, and basketball mementos, all paying tribute to Coach Wooden. As I walked up for a closer look, I noticed that among all of the memorabilia there was a plastic card.

It was one of the cards Coach Wooden had been giving out for decades: Joshua Hugh Wooden's seven-point creed.

I thought, *Coach, your dad is here today as well.*

We took our seats in Pauley Pavilion and listened as the sound system played some of Coach's favorite songs. I heard some of the same old tunes I had heard on the stereo at his Encino apartment many times: the Mills Brothers, Doris Day, Johnny Cash, and Elvis Presley. I knew that Coach himself had planned the service—the music, the speakers, the format. He had literally been planning this day for years. He wanted it to be just right—and it was.

A huge photo of Coach Wooden, along with his pyramid of success, dominated the stage. All around the arena, Coach's championship banners hung from the rafters, brilliantly illuminated by spotlights. A light also shone on one empty seat in the stands. After his retirement, Coach had always watched Bruins home games from section 103B, row 2, seat 1. The seat is now retired.

As the music played, the dignitaries and celebrities took their places in chairs on the Nell and John Wooden Court: L.A. mayor Antonio Villaraigosa, Lakers legend Jerry West, Dodgers manager Joe Torre, Yankee shortstop Derek Jeter, and Coach's former players Bill Walton, Kareem Abdul-Jabbar, Jamaal Wilkes, Swen Nater, Keith Erickson, Walt Hazzard, Gail Goodrich, Willie Naulls, and Sidney Wicks.

A big screen displayed a video of highlights from Coach Wooden's UCLA dynasty years. At eleven o'clock, legendary broadcaster Al Michaels came out to emcee the event. Michaels opened by saying, "John Wooden's life was built on an indestructible foundation." He went on to say that it was a foundation of values, character, and faith.

Michaels talked about Coach Wooden's humility and the fact that he was deeply and sincerely embarrassed whenever he was referred to as the world's greatest coach. "He didn't want to hear that," Michaels said, "but I told him, 'Coach, you have only yourself to blame for that. If you didn't want to be called the world's greatest coach, you shouldn't have gone out and won those ten national championships!'"

Coach's pastor, Dudley Rutherford, said that Coach had selected a Scripture passage as the theme of his memorial service. It was Matthew 22:34–40, in which Jesus says that the two greatest commandments are "Love the Lord your God with all your heart and with all your soul and with all your mind," and, "Love your neighbor as yourself." Love for God, love for humanity—these were the two great themes that defined Coach Wooden's life.

Pastor Rutherford asked the crowd of five thousand people, "How many of you have something that John Wooden signed for you—a book, a basketball, a game program, or his *Pyramid of Success*?" Nearly every hand went up, symbolizing the impact and influence of this one man on so many lives.

"Do you remember," Rutherford went on, "how Coach used to sit at the sidelines, clutching a rolled-up program in his hand at every game? I'd like each of you to take the program you were handed when you came here and roll it up and raise it in the air as a farewell tribute to Coach John Wooden." All around that arena, we rolled our programs and raised them high. It was a silent and moving farewell.

Kareem Abdul-Jabbar got up and spoke. "There were so many things I learned from Coach over my lifetime," he said, "but the things that mattered most were family and faith. People often ask me if Coach Wooden's reputation was for real. They ask, 'Can a coach really motivate his players without being harsh and using foul language?'

"It's the truth. He never swore at us and never talked to us about winning. Even while winning all those championships, Coach was much more concerned about having a positive effect on the lives of all the young men who played for him. Coach's value system was from another era."

Hearing that, I thought, *Absolutely true! Coach's value system came from the era of his father, Joshua Hugh Wooden.*

Longtime Dodgers broadcaster Vin Scully made a videotaped appearance, saying, "Coach kept his heart unwrinkled, and he looked to the face of God with true humility." I wondered what it meant to have an "unwrinkled" heart. Was Vin Scully saying that Coach Wooden's heart was forever young and unwrinkled by the cynicism of the times? Or was he saying that Coach's heart was like a freshly pressed suit, clean and spotless and unwrinkled? I'm not sure. Maybe all of the above.

Jamaal Wilkes told a story about Coach Wooden's underrated sense of humor. "I was selected by the Warriors with the eleventh pick of the first round of the NBA draft. There was a great deal of concern about my slender frame and whether I could hold up under all the pounding in the NBA. A sportswriter asked Coach about my chances of making it in the NBA, and he said, 'Well, he'll never pull a muscle— because there are no muscles to pull.'"

Ben Howland, who has coached the UCLA Bruins since 2003, said, "I visited John Wooden at the hospital on June 2, just two days before he died. I leaned over his bed to hug him, and it was obvious he hadn't shaved in a while. Coach said to me, 'I kind of feel like Bill Walton.'" Even on his deathbed, Coach Wooden joked about his famous contest of wills with Walton, who wanted to bend Coach's rules and grow a beard.

Keith Erickson also spoke. "John Wooden," he said, "was honest, wise, humble, fun, kind, gentle, filled with faith—and Jesus Christ was the Lord of his life. I visited Coach at his condo a few weeks before he passed away, and I asked him how he wanted to be remembered. He told me, 'As a man who came as close to being the man my father was.'" Then, choking back tears, Keith added, "Coach, your father would be very proud of you."

The program closed with a nineteen-minute video with photos and highlights of Coach Wooden's entire life, from birth to age ninety-nine. It closed with Coach reciting a poem he had written, which included these lines:

> Though I know down here my time is short,
> There is endless time up there
> And He will forgive and keep me
> Forever in His loving care.

The video ended with a portrait of Coach and the words his father had given him: "Make each day your masterpiece."

As the lights came up, we heard the opening lines of "Over the Rainbow," the light and happy calypso version. "Somewhere over the rainbow, way up high . . ." I wish I'd had the Kleenex concession at Pauley Pavilion that day! There were no dry eyes in the place—including mine. After "Over the Rainbow," Louis Armstrong sang "What a Wonderful World," perfectly capturing Coach's spirit of optimism and love for humanity.

The service was over. People reluctantly got up from their seats, but no one wanted to leave. We all just wanted to remain there together, remembering Coach, listening to the music he loved, drinking in the last few moments of that celebration.

Finally, Ken and I walked out of Pauley Pavilion, got in Ken's car, went to Houston's to enjoy lunch together, and then took the Santa Monica Freeway east. The Yankees were in town to play the Dodgers, and I had arranged to get tickets for us both. So Ken and I went out to Dodger Stadium to watch the game at 4 p.m.

We both needed that. After an emotionally intense morning, after all the memories and tears, we needed to sit in the stands with fifty thousand other fans, yelling and munching Cracker Jack like a couple of kids.

As Ken and I watched the game, we got a seven-foot-two-inch confirmation that we'd made the right choice, for who should we see in the aisle in front of us but Kareem Abdul-Jabbar himself! Kareem knew: This was what Coach would want us to do. He didn't want people to mourn. He wanted everyone to celebrate his life, to celebrate their own lives, to celebrate *all* of life.

Somewhere, over the rainbow . . . what a wonderful world . . .

I looked up into the sky, and I could feel Coach smiling down on us. I could see the twinkle in his eyes. I could even hear his voice.

Life goes on. *Enjoy the game.*

Make this day—this life—your masterpiece.

Appendix 1

Coach Wooden's Legendary Record

John Robert Wooden

October 10, 1910–June 4, 2010

W hen Coach John Wooden announced his retirement after the 1974–75 season, he concluded a forty-year career as a head coach, including twenty-seven years as head coach of the UCLA Bruins. His career win-loss record of 885–203 (a .813 career percentage) is unequaled. His record with the Bruins is 620–147. Under Coach Wooden, the Bruins amassed an unprecedented ten NCAA championships, including seven consecutive championships from 1967 to 1973.

Coach Wooden's Bruins also achieved two of the most amazing winning streaks in all of sports: eighty-eight consecutive wins over four seasons (including two undefeated 30–0 seasons, 1971–72 and 1972–73) and thirty-eight consecutive NCAA tournament wins. Coach Wooden's UCLA Bruins achieved a record of 149–2 at UCLA's Pauley Pavilion. In all, Wooden coached his Bruins to four 30–0 undefeated seasons and nineteen conference championships.

Coach Wooden was honored as a charter member of the NABC National Basketball Hall of Fame, the Pac-10 Basketball Hall of Honor, and the UCLA Athletics Hall of Fame. He was the first person inducted into the Naismith Memorial Basketball Hall of Fame as both player and coach. In 2003, Coach Wooden received the Presidential Medal of Freedom (the highest honor awarded to a civilian) from President George W. Bush at a White House ceremony. On July 29, 2009, the *Sporting News* named Coach Wooden the Greatest Coach of All Time in any sport, college or professional.

Coach Wooden was married for fifty-three years to his wife, Nell, who died on March 21, 1985. He celebrated his ninety-ninth birthday on October 14, 2009. On June 4, 2010, Coach Wooden died of natural causes at the Ronald Reagan UCLA Medical Center. He is survived by a son, James Hugh Wooden; a daughter, Nancy Anne Wooden; and seven grandchildren and thirteen great-grandchildren.

He leaves behind a legacy of faith, values, and character and a legend of accomplishment that will never be equaled.

The John Wooden Legend

High School Coaching Record—11 Seasons
(two seasons at Dayton High School, Dayton, Kentucky; nine seasons at Central High School, South Bend, Indiana)

Won	Lost	Percentage
218	42	.838

Coaching Record at Indiana State University—2 Seasons

Won	Lost	Percentage
44	15	.778

Coaching Record at UCLA—27 Seasons (Conference Record)

Won	Lost	Percentage
316	68	.823

Coaching Record at UCLA—27 Seasons (Full Season Record)

Won	Lost	Percentage
620	147	.808

Forty-Season Career Coaching Record

Won	Lost	Percentage
885	203	.813

Season by Season at Indiana State and UCLA

Season	School	W–L	Percentage	NCAA Tournament
1946–47	Indiana St.	17–8	.680	
1947–48	Indiana St.	27–7	.794	
1948–49	UCLA	22–7	.759	
1949–50	UCLA	24–7	.774	0–2 in NCAA Tourney
1950–51	UCLA	19–10	.655	
1951–52	UCLA	19–12	.613	0–2 in NCAA Tourney
1952–53	UCLA	16–8	.667	
1953–54	UCLA	18–7	.720	
1954–55	UCLA	21–5	.808	
1955–56	UCLA	22–6	.786	1–1 in NCAA Tourney
1956–57	UCLA	22–4	.846	
1957–58	UCLA	16–10	.615	
1958–59	UCLA	16–9	.640	

Season	School	W–L	Percentage	NCAA Tournament
1959–60	UCLA	14–12	.538	
1960–61	UCLA	18–8	.692	
1961–62	UCLA	18–11	.621	2–2, finished 4th in NCAA Tourney
1962–63	UCLA	20–9	.690	0–2 in NCAA Tourney
1963–64	UCLA	30–0	1.000	4–0 NCAA Champions
1964–65	UCLA	28–2	.933	4–0 NCAA Champions
1965–66	UCLA	18–8	.692	
1966–67	UCLA	30–0	1.000	4–0 NCAA Champions
1967–68	UCLA	29–1	.967	4–0 NCAA Champions
1968–69	UCLA	29–1	.967	4–0 NCAA Champions
1969–70	UCLA	28–2	.933	4–0 NCAA Champions
1970–71	UCLA	29–1	.967	4–0 NCAA Champions
1971–72	UCLA	30–0	1.000	4–0 NCAA Champions
1972–73	UCLA	30–0	1.000	4–0 NCAA Champions
1973–74	UCLA	26–4	.867	3–1, finished 3rd in NCAA Tourney
1974–75	UCLA	28–3	.903	5–0 NCAA Champions

The Ten Championship Seasons

1964 UCLA defeats Duke 98–83

Regional Semifinals—West	UCLA 95, Seattle 90
Regional Finals—West	UCLA 76, San Francisco 72
National Semifinals	UCLA 90, Kansas State 84
National Championship	UCLA 98, Duke 83

1965 UCLA defeats Michigan 91–80

Regional Semifinals—West	UCLA 100, Brigham Young 76
Regional Finals—West	UCLA 101, San Francisco 93
National Semifinals	UCLA 108, Wichita State 89
National Championship	UCLA 91, Michigan 80

1967 UCLA defeats Dayton 79–64

Regional Semifinals—West	UCLA 109, Wyoming 60
Regional Finals—West	UCLA 80, Pacific 64
National Semifinals	UCLA 73, Houston 58
National Championship	UCLA 79, Dayton 64

1968 UCLA defeats North Carolina 78–55

Regional Semifinals—West	UCLA 58, New Mexico State 49
Regional Finals—West	UCLA 87, Santa Clara 66
National Semifinals	UCLA 101, Houston 69
National Championship	UCLA 78, North Carolina 55

1969 UCLA defeats Purdue 92–72

Regional Semifinals—West	UCLA 53, New Mexico State 38
Regional Finals—West	UCLA 90, Santa Clara 52
National Semifinals	UCLA 85, Drake 82
National Championship	UCLA 92, Purdue 72

1970 UCLA defeats Jacksonville 80–69

Regional Semifinals—West	UCLA 88, Long Beach State 65
Regional Finals—West	UCLA 101, Utah State 79
National Semifinals	UCLA 93, New Mexico State 77
National Championship	UCLA 80, Jacksonville 69

1971 UCLA defeats Villanova 68–62

Regional Semifinals—West	UCLA 91, Brigham Young 73
Regional Finals—West	UCLA 57, Long Beach State 55
National Semifinals	UCLA 68, Kansas 60
National Championship	UCLA 68, Villanova 62

1972 UCLA defeats Florida State 81–76

Regional Semifinals—West	UCLA 90, Weber State 58
Regional Finals—West	UCLA 73, Long Beach State 57
National Semifinals	UCLA 96, Louisville 77
National Championship	UCLA 81, Florida State 76

1973 UCLA defeats Memphis 87–66

Regional Semifinals—West	UCLA 98, Arizona State 81
Regional Finals—West	UCLA 54, San Francisco 39
National Semifinals	UCLA 70, Indiana 59
National Championship	UCLA 87, Memphis State 66

1975 UCLA defeats Kentucky 92–85

First Round—West	UCLA 103, Michigan 91 (OT)
Regional Semifinals—West	UCLA 67, Montana 64
Regional Finals—West	UCLA 89, Arizona State 75
National Semifinals	UCLA 75, Louisville 74 (OT)
National Championship	UCLA 92, Kentucky 85

Appendix 2

Woodenisms

Coach John Wooden taught the game of life. The victories and championships on the basketball court were mere by-product. One of Coach's most effective teaching methods was to distill great truths into sayings or maxims (as his father did in the seven-point creed). Those maxims have come to be known as "Woodenisms." Here is a selection of Coach Wooden's most memorable maxims.

ACCOMPLISHMENT (ACHIEVEMENT)

Don't measure yourself by what you have accomplished but by what you should have accomplished with your ability.

ACTION

Be quick, but don't hurry.
Never mistake activity for achievement.
It isn't what you do but how you do it.

ADVERSITY

Adversity is the state in which man most easily becomes acquainted with himself, being especially free of admirers then.

ATTITUDE

Things turn out best for the people who make the best of the way things turn out.

Don't let what you cannot do interfere with what you can do.

BOOKS

The worst thing about new books is that they keep us from reading the old ones.

CHARACTER

Winning takes talent, to repeat takes character.

Ability may get you to the top, but it takes character to keep you there.

Be more concerned with your character than your reputation, because your character is what you *really* are, while your reputation is merely what others *think* you are.

What you are as a person is far more important than what you are as a basketball player.

COACHING

A coach is someone who can give correction without causing resentment.

COMPETITIVE SPIRIT

It's not so important who starts the game but who finishes it.

DISCIPLINE

Discipline yourself and others won't need to.

EXCELLENCE

If you don't have time to do it right, when will you have time to do it over?

It's the little details that are vital. Little things make big things happen.

FAILURE AND MISTAKES

Failure is not fatal, but failure to change might be.

If you're not making mistakes, then you're not doing anything. I'm positive that a doer makes mistakes.

LEARNING

Learn as if you were to live forever. Live as if you were to die tomorrow.

It is what you learn after you know it all that counts.

MONEY

Don't let making a living prevent you from making a life.

OTHERS

You have not lived a perfect day until you've done something for somebody who cannot repay you.

Consider the rights of others before your own feelings and the feelings of others before your own rights.

PRAISE AND CRITICISM

You can't let praise or criticism get to you. It's a weakness to get caught up in either one.

PREPARATION

Failure to prepare is preparing to fail.

RIGHT AND WRONG

What is right is more important than who is right.

SUCCESS

Success is peace of mind, which is a direct result of self-satisfaction in knowing you made the effort to become the best of which you are capable.

Success is never final; failure is never fatal. It's courage that counts.

TALENT

I'd rather have a lot of talent and a little experience than a lot of experience and a little talent.

Ability is a poor man's wealth.

TEAMWORK

Much can be accomplished by teamwork when no one is concerned about who gets credit.

The main ingredient of stardom is the rest of the team.

A player who makes the team great is better than a great player.

The best way to improve the team is to improve yourself.

Notes

Introduction: Well Done, Coach

1. John Wooden with Steve Jamison, *My Personal Best: Life Lessons from an All-American Journey* (New York: McGraw-Hill, 2004), 4.
2. Ibid., 204.

Chapter 1: A Common Man, a Leader's Leader

1. John Wooden and Don Yaeger, *A Game Plan for Life: The Power of Mentoring* (New York: Bloomsbury, 2009), 13.
2. John Wooden and Jay Carty, *Coach Wooden One-on-One* (Ventura, CA: Regal Books, 2003), entry for Day 9, "The Blessing."
3. Wooden and Jamison, *My Personal Best*, 1.
4. Ibid., 8.
5. Ibid., 8–9.
6. Wooden and Yaeger, *Game Plan for Life*, 23.
7. Wooden and Jamison, *My Personal Best*, 9.
8. Wooden and Yaeger, *Game Plan for Life*, 23.
9. Wooden and Jamison, *My Personal Best*, 4.
10. John Wooden, "Interview: John Wooden, Basketball's Coaching Legend," February 27, 1996, Los Angeles, California, Academy of Achievement website, www.achievement.org/autodoc/printmember/woo0int-1.
11. Seth Davis, "Breakfast with John Wooden: Bruins Coach Ben Howland Benefits from Wizard of Westwood's Wisdom," November 3, 2003, http://sportsillustrated.cnn.com/vault/article/web/COM1033363/index.htm.
12. Wooden and Yaeger, *Game Plan for Life*, 14.
13. Neville L. Johnson, *The John Wooden Pyramid of Success: The Authorized Biography, Philosophy, and Ultimate Guide to Life, Leadership, Friendship, and*

Love of the Greatest Coach in the History of Sports, rev. ed. (Los Angeles: Cool Titles, 2003), 12.

Chapter 2: Be True to Yourself

1. Adam de Jong, "The Soul of UCLA, On- and Off-Court," *Daily Bruin*, October 19, 2005, http://dailybruin.ucla.edu/stories/2005/oct/19/ithe-soul-of-ucla-on-and-off-c/.

2. John R. Wooden with Steve Jamison, *Wooden: A Lifetime of Observations and Reflections On and Off the Court* (Chicago: Contemporary Books, 1997), 9–10.

3. William Shakespeare, *The Tragedy of Hamlet, Prince of Denmark*, Act I, Scene III, *The Harvard Classics* (New York: P.F. Collier & Son, 1909–1914), Bartelby.com, 2001, www.bartleby.com/46/2/13.html.

4. Ibid.

5. Ibid.

6. Ira Berkow, "West Point Is Standing at Attention for Army Women's Coach," *New York Times*, March 15, 2006, www.nytimes.com/2006/03/15/sports/sportsspecial1/15dixon.html?_r=1&ei=5070&en=3aa182aece3d25b4&ex=1143090000&adxnnl=1&emc=eta1&adxnnlx=1142425879–MppVwxvIMhREHjc1DEa6aA; Associated Press, "Autopsy Shows Dixon Had Enlarged Heart," ESPN Online, April 14, 2006, http://sports.espn.go.com/ncw/news/story?id=2400335.

7. Wooden and Jamison, *My Personal Best*, 4–5.

8. Andrew Hill with John Wooden, *Be Quick—but Don't Hurry: Finding Success in the Teachings of a Lifetime* (New York: Simon & Schuster, 2001), 26.

9. Rick Reilly, "Life of Reilly: One Coach Still Knows More Than All the Others Combined; and He's Been Retired for Three Decades," *ESPN Magazine*, October 29, 2008, http://sports.espn.go.com/espnmag/story?section=magazine&id=3669154.

10. Pat Williams with David Wimbish, *How to Be like Coach Wooden: Life Lessons from Basketball's Greatest Leader* (Deerfield Beach, FL: Health Communications, Inc., 2006), 16–17.

11. William Safire and Leonard Safir, *Words of Wisdom: More Good Advice* (New York: Simon & Schuster, 1990), 102.

12. Wooden and Jamison, *Wooden*, 58.

13. Ibid., 40.

14. John Blaydes, *The Educator's Book of Quotes* (Thousand Oaks, CA: Corwin Press, 2003), 150.

Chapter 3: Help Others

1. Wooden and Jamison, *Wooden*, 9–10.

2. Williams and Wimbish, *How to Be like Coach Wooden*, 15.

3. Ibid.

4. Ibid.

5. Steve Wulf, "Murphy's Law Is Nice Guys Finish First," *Sports Illustrated*, July 4, 1983, http://sportsillustrated.cnn.com/vault/article/magazine/MAG1120992/

index.htm; and David Whitley, "Murphy Swings Away at Steroids in Our Pastime," *Orlando Sentinel*, June 24, 2007, http://articles.orlandosentinel.com/2007–06–24/sports/WHITLEY24_1_dale-murphy-murphy-law-cheat.

6. "Cheerleading: The Dallas Cowboy Cheerleaders—Sassy but Classy," *Newsweek*, October 25, 1999, "Sports Highlights of the '70s," www.superseventies.com/sports.html.

7. Dave Thomas, founder, Wendy's International, "What Makes for Success?," July 1996, Hillsdale College *Imprimis*, www.hillsdale.edu/news/imprimis/archive/issue.asp?year=1996&month=07; St. Jude Children's Research Hospital, "Danny's Promise," www.stjude.org/stjude/v/index.jsp?vgnextoid=576bfa2454e70110VgnVCM1000001e0215acRCRD&vgnextchannel=5af213c016118010VgnVCM1000000e2015acRCRD; Abny Santicola, "Star Power: When Newly Successful Actor Danny Thomas Founded ALSAC/St. Jude Children's Research Hospital 50 Years Ago, He Started a Hollywood Fundraising Connection That Still Shines Today," FundRaisingSuccessMag.com, June 1, 2007, www.fundraisingsuccessmag.com/story/story.bsp?sid=56707&var=story; and Gary L. Lisman and Arlene Parr, *Bittersweet Memories: A History of the Peoria State Hospital* (Victoria, BC: Trafford Publishing, 2005), 241–42.

8. Danny Thomas Quotes, ThinkExist.com, http://thinkexist.com/quotation/all_of_us_are_born_for_a_reason-but_all_of_us_don/339486.html.

9. Marlo Thomas Quotes, ThinkExist.com, http://thinkexist.com/quotation/my-father-said-there-were-two-kinds-of-people-in/411391.html.

10. John Wooden with Jack Tobin, *They Call Me Coach* (New York: McGraw-Hill, 1988), 26.

11. John Wooden, "Coach!" *UCLA Magazine*, Summer 2000, www.magazine.ucla.edu/year2000/summer00_01_7.html.

12. Ibid.

13. Wooden and Yaeger, *A Game Plan for Life*, 16.

Chapter 4: Make Each Day Your Masterpiece

1. Jim Denney, *Answers to Satisfy the Soul* (Sanger, CA: Quill Driver Books, 2001), 43.

2. Bob Vorwald, *What It Means to Be a Cub: The North Side's Greatest Players Talk about Cubs Baseball* (Chicago: Triumph Books, 2010), 223–24.

3. Wooden and Jamison, *Wooden*, 11–12.

4. Valorie Kondos Field, "Ask the Bruins—Valorie Kondos Field," UCLABruins.com, February 23, 2007, www.uclabruins.com/sports/w-gym/spec-rel/022307aaa.html.

5. Editorial, "Be Like Laich," *USA Today*, May 2, 2010, www.usatoday.com/news/opinion/editorials/2010–05–03–editorial03_ST3_N.htm.

Chapter 5: Drink Deeply from Good Books, Especially the Bible

1. Wooden and Jamison, *Wooden*, 12.

2. Wooden and Jamison, *My Personal Best*, 3.

3. Lilless McPherson Shilling and Linda K. Fuller, *Dictionary of Quotations in Communications* (Santa Barbara, CA: Greenwood, 1997), 30.

4. Charles W. Eliot, *The Happy Life* (New York: Thomas Y. Crowell & Co., 1896), 23.

5. Gerald J. Prokopowicz, *Did Lincoln Own Slaves? and Other Frequently Asked Questions about Abraham Lincoln* (New York: Random House, 2008), 22.

6. Alex Ayers, *The Wit and Wisdom of Mark Twain* (New York: HarperCollins, 1987), 26.

7. "About Coach Dale Brown," CoachDaleBrownSpeaks.com, May 29, 2009, www.coachdalebrownspeaks.com/index.php?option=com_content&view=article&id=69&Itemid=100.

8. William Safire, *Lend Me Your Ears: Great Speeches in History*, rev. ed. (New York: Norton, 2004), 611–12.

9. Robert Andrews, *The Columbia Dictionary of Quotations* (New York: Columbia University Press, 1993), 103.

10. "Victoria's Quotes," Goodreads.com, www.goodreads.com/quotes/list/2299764–victoria.

11. Jonathan Frye, "Leadership Tips from Bill Gates," LeadershipJot.com, October 6, 2008, www.leadershipjot.com/2008/10/06/leadership-tips-from-bill-gates/.

12. United Nations University, "3 Hydro-Powered Reverse-Osmosis Desalination in Water-Resources Development in Kuwait," UNU.edu, www.unu.edu/unupress/unupbooks/80858e/80858E0b.htm.

13. Peter Kylling, "The Borrowers," CBarks.dk, April 19, 2005, www.cbarks.dk/theborrowers.htm; and Pat Williams, *Go for the Magic* (Nashville: Thomas Nelson, 1998), 91.

14. Pat Williams with Peggy Matthews-Rose, *Read for Your Life* (Deerfield Beach, FL: Health Communications, Inc., 2007), 83–84; Elizabeth Kiem, "Debbie Ryan Looms as a Giant in Women's Basketball," Inside UVA, August 2002, www.virginia.edu/insideuva/2002/06/ryan.html; and Sal Ruibal, "Fighting Cancer Is a New Mission for Armstrong," *USA Today*, July 25, 2005, www.usatoday.com/sports/cycling/tourdefrance/2005-07-24-armstrong-mission_x.htm.

15. Charlie "Tremendous" Jones, "Postcards from My Son," excerpted from the Special Teenager Session at the Jim Rohn Weekend Seminar "Excelling in the New Millennium," Team Victory website, www.team-victory.com/Motivational_Stories/CJ_Postcards.asp.

16. Ibid.

Chapter 6: Make Friendship a Fine Art

1. Wooden and Tobin, *They Call Me Coach*, 67.

2. Johnson, *The John Wooden Pyramid of Success*, 114.

3. Wooden and Jamison, *Wooden*, 12–13.

4. John Wooden with Jay Carty, *Coach Wooden's Pyramid of Success Playbook* (Ventura, CA: Regal Books, 2005), 15.

5. Cyril Charney, *The Portable Mentor: Your Anywhere, Anytime Career Coach and Problem Solver* (New York: AMACOM, 2004), 157.

6. Geoffrey Greif, *The Buddy System: Understanding Male Friendships* (New York: Oxford, 2009), 41.

7. Larry Chang, *Wisdom for the Soul: Five Millennia of Prescriptions for Spiritual Healing* (Washington, DC: Gnosophia Publishers, 2006), 326.

8. Ibid.

9. Henri J. M. Nouwen, *Out of Solitude: Three Meditations on the Christian Life* (Notre Dame, IN: Ave Maria Press, 2004), 38.

10. Bob Dole, *Great Presidential Wit* (New York: Touchstone, 2002), 33.

11. Peter Boulware with Roxanne Robbins, "We Helped Each Other Make Wise Choices," *Connection: The Good News Magazine*, January 1999, www.connectionmagazine.org/archives_old/archives/1999/january/helpeachother.htm.

12. Wooden and Carty, *Coach Wooden One-on-One*, entry for Day 58, "Breaking Ties."

13. Ibid., entry for Day 5, "Such a Time as This."

Chapter 7: Build a Shelter against a Rainy Day by the Life You Live

1. Williams and Wimbish, *How to Be like Coach Wooden*, 15.

2. Jim O'Connell, "'Wizard of Westwood' Holds Dreams of UCLA's Glorious Past," *Park City Daily News*, March 29, 1995, 1B–2B.

3. Wooden and Jamison, *Wooden*, 13.

4. Dennis Sargent and Martha Sargent, *Retire—and Start Your Own Business: Five Steps to Success* (Berkeley, CA: Nolo, 2008), 30.

5. Wooden and Jamison, *Wooden*, 42.

6. Michael Richmond, *The Redskins Encyclopedia* (Philadelphia: Temple University Press, 2008), 236.

7. John Wooden, interview, "John Wooden: Values, Victory, and Peace of Mind," KQED-TV, March 14, 2010, www.livedash.com/transcript/john_wooden__values,_victory_and_peace_of_mind/918/KQED/Sunday_March_14_2010/172091/.

8. George W. Sinquefield, "Running the Christian Race," www.our.home withgod.com/sinque/Sermon64.html.

9. Denney, *Answers to Satisfy the Soul*, 23.

10. Wooden and Jamison, *Wooden*, 13.

11. Wooden and Tobin, *They Call Me Coach*, 94.

12. Johnson, *The John Wooden Pyramid of Success*, 192.

13. Wooden and Jamison, *My Personal Best*, 31–35.

Chapter 8: Pray for Guidance and Counsel, and Give Thanks for Your Blessings Each Day

1. Mitch Borowitz, "From the Socks Up: The Extraordinary Coaching Life of John Wooden," November 2004, MitchHorowitz.com, www.mitchhorowitz.com/john-wooden.html.

2. Wooden and Tobin, *They Call Me Coach*, 69.

3. Wooden and Jamison, *Wooden*, 14.

4. Jan Karon, *A New Song* (New York: Penguin, 2000), 317.

5. Thomas Lickona, *Character Matters* (New York: Simon & Schuster, 2004), 10.

6. Melody Beattie, *The Language of Letting Go* (Center City, MN: Hazelden Publishing, 1990), 218.

7. Vincent J. Dooley with Tony Barnhart, *Dooley: My Forty Years at Georgia* (Chicago: Triumph Books, 2005), 3–4.

8. Wooden and Jamison, *Wooden*, 14.

9. Wooden and Tobin, *They Call Me Coach*, 95.

10. Ibid.

You can contact Pat Williams at:

Pat Williams
c/o Orlando Magic
8701 Maitland Summit Boulevard
Orlando, FL 32810
phone: 407-916-2404
pwilliams@orlandomagic.com

Visit Pat Williams's website at:

www.PatWilliamsMotivate.com

If you would like to set up a speaking engagement for Pat Williams, please call or write his assistant, Andrew Herdliska, at the above address, or call him at 407-916-2401. Requests can also be faxed to 407-916-2986 or emailed to aherdliska@ orlandomagic.com.

We would love to hear from you. Please send your comments about this book to Pat Williams at the above address. Thank you.

Be the First
to Hear about
Other New Books
from Revell!

Sign up for announcements about
new and upcoming titles at

www.revellbooks.com/signup

Follow us on
RevellBooks

Don't miss out on our
great reads!

R
Revell
a division of Baker Publishing Group
www.RevellBooks.com